IF IT IS TO BE
IT'S UP
TO ME

How *to* Develop
the Attitude *of*
a Winner
and Become
a Leader

THOMAS B. SMITH

If It Is To Be
It's Up To Me

Thomas B. Smith
Copyright©2001 by Thomas B. Smith
e-mail: wasp7646@aol.com
ISBN 0-938716-43-3

Published by
Possibility Press
e-mail: PossPress@excite.com

Manufactured in the United States of America

Other Books by *Possibility Press*

Tapes by *Possibility Press*

Dedication

This book is dedicated to my positive, enthusiastic, always cheerful wife, Debby, who made many sacrifices during my years of leading an insurance agency and in research and writing.

Acknowledgements

Special thanks to my daughters, Judy and Kathy, who typed the original manuscript.

I acknowledge that the motivation for this work came from many friends, professional associates, community co-workers, and my church. Thanks to all for your inspiration and wisdom.

I acknowledge and appreciate the wisdom and guidance of my editors and publisher, and everyone else on their staff who has contributed to making this book what it is.

I have had too many mentors to mention. They have contributed to my attitude, optimism, and enthusiasm. My sincerest thanks to you all!

Also, thank you God, for the opportunity to share this information.

Contents

Introduction

The "Good Old Days"

*"I like the dreams of the future better than the
history of the past."*
Thomas Jefferson

Humble Beginnings...

My birthplace, Rocky Hill, New Jersey, in the United States,
had a population of only 500 when I was born in 1926. It was hit
hard by the stock market crash of 1929 and the Great Depression
that followed, which lasted through most of the next decade.

The Atlantic Terra Cotta plant, the only industry in town,
closed—throwing 300 men and women into the growing ranks of
the unemployed. My father, who had struggled for many years to
buy a home for his ever growing family (I was number eight of
eleven!), was among those laid off. As a result, we lost our
modest home and moved into a rented one a few miles away.

Dad was a self-educated, hardworking man who always gave
his best to everything he did. In addition to his full-time job, he
raised chickens to supply an egg route he had started in and
around Princeton, New Jersey.

After Dad lost his job, our family survived with the income
from the egg route, until he found another job with Princeton
University. With eight young mouths to feed, he had a tough
time. However, as the old cliché goes, *"When the going gets*

tough, the tough get going. " That's my dad. He just kept going—no matter what happened.

Battered Self-Esteem

My four older brothers teased me incessantly during the first 14 or so years of my life. As a result, my self-esteem (self-respect), as a child, was rather beat-up. Later in life, I learned that self-esteem is essential to a person's well being and success. Fortunately, I was able to build up my self-esteem as I gained knowledge and matured, by doing my best to maintain a positive attitude.

I learned to be assertive as a youngster because to get what I wanted, I had to compete with my brothers. Otherwise, they would've run all over me! These traits eventually paid off, as I entered the adult world and the workplace.

Rich in Love and Valuable Lessons

I often remark to my friends, when we start talking about the "good old days" that, while I was growing up, our family was so poor that the Depression came and went and we hardly knew the difference!

Our Christmas seasons were quite bleak and bare, in terms of gifts, that is. One year I recall receiving a small red fire truck. It was given to me after the Princeton, New Jersey Lion's Club annual Christmas movie at the Garden Theater. The movie was free and toys were distributed to all the children present.

For the next few years, I wrapped this same little fire truck, put it under the small tree my brothers had cut down and dragged in from the woods, then unwrapped it as my only present!

My parents read the Bible with us daily and taught us the Ten Commandments. An important principle I learned, early in life, was the Golden Rule—"Do unto others as you would have others do unto you." This has stayed with me throughout my life and has paid off handsomely.

I also learned that "God helps those who help themselves." I have always followed this concept and taught it to my children and business and civic associates.

A Firm Foundation

I sincerely believe that the training my parents gave me set the stage for my success in life. I learned that hard work produces results, and that you need to work smart, too, usually following the guidance of someone who already is where you want to be. You need to do your best, which means doing whatever's necessary to accomplish what you set out to do.

It led me to be a doer rather than just a talker, to be confident, and moving forward in my thinking and actions, and to have a positive attitude about every aspect of my life and in my relationships with others.

Rich in Values

My parents were strong disciplinarians. We were taught to be honest, not only in dealing with others, but also with ourselves. We were not allowed to shirk our responsibilities—especially to our family. We were taught to have respect for other people's property, ideas, and values. We were reminded of these teachings by being disciplined whenever we were deficient in these areas!

Because I felt a strong desire to earn money to help my family, I dropped out of high school after my sophomore year. In looking back, this was the first and only time I had ever quit on anything. However, at the time, even though my grades were above average, it seemed like the best thing to do. (I certainly wouldn't recommend doing this today, because, for some, not only could it be a poor move career or business-wise, it could set up a pattern of quitting in life.)

Learning the Value of Commitment and Consistent Action

After my discharge from the military following World War II, I re-enrolled in high school. I completed the requirements in one year by doubling up on required courses. This experience helped to teach me that—*commitment and consistent action toward a worthwhile goal can pay huge dividends*. Of course you also need to work smart, otherwise, you could end up "spinning your wheels" like a hamster running in a circular cage—moving fast, but going nowhere!

Early Lesson in Leadership

After graduation, I worked for two years to save money to go to a small business college in New England. During my first semester I wanted to participate in student government. However I had a rather strong difference of opinion with a senior student who had run things his way the previous year.

We had different philosophies about what direction and impact the student body would have in the administration of the college. And we also disagreed about each other's approach to leadership.

He was an autocratic leader, who insisted he had the best ideas and everything had to be done his way. I was a participative leader, who looked for ideas from others and worked with and through them.

Carefrontation

The wonderful result of our confrontations was that we understood and respected one another and became close friends. Ironically he was my best man when I got married a year later! I learned from this challenging relationship.

For example, when you carefront (kindly confront) someone concerning your feelings about their behavior and you do it in a non-attacking manner, it causes your relationship to go to a new level. The courage it takes to carefront someone is definitely worth it. Otherwise, the relationship is usually stuck because of nonproductive behavior patterns, and often doomed to fail.

A Budding Sales Leader

Because I needed the money, I bid for and received the contract to operate the college bookstore. I enjoyed this responsibility. Fortunately for me, a large capital investment wasn't required, because I didn't have rent to pay, and I didn't need employees.

I was able to afford to stock the items I thought would sell and had full control of the operation. Since we were located only five miles from a major supplier, I didn't have much money tied-up in inventory.

I enjoyed sales in the bookstore, as well as in my building supply sales job just before college. This convinced me my future was in sales and sales leadership.

After I graduated from college, I accepted a position as a sales representative with a large insurance company. I took to the insurance business like a duck takes to water. I worked hard and studied long hours. My income rose to levels I hadn't even dreamed of. This reinforced something I had learned as a teenager. *Honest, intelligent effort is always rewarded.*

I did extremely well in insurance sales for a number of reasons. I had a sense of mission—a purpose. I developed the ability to quickly establish a reputation for reliable and prompt service. I also focused a great deal of attention on understanding people's individual insurance needs. Being committed to excellence and to being a good student of the business—I eagerly absorbed and put into practice the training I received. This gave me more knowledge to better serve my clients.

Keep Growing Yourself

The insurance business changed over the years. New products and concepts were developed that required many hours of study and research. Some of the older agents often asked me if I'd like to go back to the good old days when the business was easier to understand. My response was, "No way!" I welcomed the changes, which, generally speaking, were advantageous to my customers. Constant improvement is a mainstay of a cutting edge company.

Just as a company needs to be always fine-tuning and perhaps adding to their line of products and services, we all need to be personally developing ourselves, increasing our knowledge and improving our skills. A steady diet of continuing education is a key ingredient to your success. It helps you grow and improve your self-confidence and self-esteem—to better enable you to build your business or profession. Growth is a prerequisite for continued success and the only way you can coast is downhill.

Success is a journey not a destination. So keep developing yourself, following your mentor's or leader's recommendations, and enjoy the trip. There is no such thing as maintaining a status quo because time marches on. It waits for no one. You're either going backward or moving on. We all need to do something with our time, so let's do something toward our dreams and goals.

After four years of developing and growing as an agent, I moved into leadership, where I stayed for the balance of my 34 year career. Part of the key to my successes has been the strong work ethic I developed during my childhood and teenage years. My actions were based on my values and what I perceived to be the right thing to do. Certainly I made mistakes. But I consistently gave my best effort and maintained integrity, with myself and those I served.

Testing My Positive Attitude and Leadership Ability

Having a great attitude is central to your reaching your goals. Everything you do reflects your attitude toward yourself and others.

As the new leader of an agency that had been rated lowest in productivity among 400 agencies nationwide, I had a challenge on my hands! This would put my positive attitude and skills to the test. My agents and unit managers looked to me for leadership.

It was not a matter of do as I say, but do as I do. In addition to providing training and leadership to my agents, I was a working leader. I did my share of production to set a good example and help our agency dig itself out of the hole of its extremely poor reputation. We all got in there, "dirtying our hands" and, as a team, pulled together to create new results.

My main goal was to create an environment that was conducive to success. So I set out to increase the morale and upgrade the knowledge of my associates so they could raise their self-confidence and self-esteem. I made a commitment to help each of them reach their goals.

This all resulted in a 50 percent increase in productivity during our first year together and a hefty increase in income for my people. The key is to help other people get what they want. When you help enough of them, you'll get what you want! Support others in achieving their dreams, and you're more likely to make *your* dreams a reality.

During my career as an agency leader, we dug the office out of its slump to rank in the top 20 percent nationally and were able to maintain that level of success. I'm particularly pleased and gratified by the contributions my associates made to the financial security of their clients, friends, and families.

As you continue to reach out to others, in your career or business, you're likely to also feel quite good about yourself, those you're working with, and the clients or customers your serving, as well, because of the positive difference you're making in all those people's lives.

As a result of putting people first, our agency was extremely profitable to our company, our agents, as well as to our policyholders. Everybody won! For you to win, put people before products and services. Care about your associates and others you're helping, as well as those who are users or potential users of your products and services.

I credit much of my success to those who helped me along the way. I encourage you to enlist the help of a mentor or leader to guide you and believe in you as you move toward your dreams.

Remember, it doesn't matter what your financial situation is, what you have achieved so far, how old or young you are, what your environment is, your current lifestyle, your nationality, or your educational level. You can improve everything in your life with a positive attitude, determination, commitment, and doing whatever it takes to make it happen.

In the following chapters you'll learn how having a positive attitude affects your personal and business life, including your health. You'll also learn how to be an effective leader so you can build your business or profession and achieve your goals and dreams.

Look to yourself, that person in the mirror, to take action and turn dreams into things you have done. You are cast as the main character in the script of your life. Yes, *you!* Now is the time to go forward in faith. Follow your dreams and they'll take you where you need to go. Remember, as the title of this book says— *if it is to be, it's up to me.*

Chapter One

How Is Your Attitude?

*"Many times the difference between whether you achieve
your goals or not is your attitude."*

Attitude, Attitude, Attitude

You've probably been told that your attitude is important to your success. So first of all, let's define this commonly-discussed word: Attitude is your mood, reflection, feelings, position, or idea, shown by your facial expression, posture of your body, tone of voice, words, and actions. You may be saying, "This is all well and good, but..."

What's the Big Deal About Being Positive?

An optimistic outlook on life has many advantages. It means you're solution-oriented and a possibility thinker. You look for the good. When you have a positive attitude, you're more likely to be committed and achieve your goals and dreams. For example, in your profession or business, as well as in your personal life, you'll attract more positive thinking people to associate with.

You're on an upward spiral—your life keeps getting better and better. You're more likely to be happy, healthy, and successful in all areas of your life. Your optimism will help you love life, take positive actions, and make some great things happen.

During my career as a leader, I discovered there are basically three types of people:

- ◆ Those who make things happen.
- ◆ Those who watch things happen.
- ◆ Those who don't know what's happening.

Where do you fit in? Remember, it's never too late to change your attitude. You may need to evict a negative attitude that has been bogging you down—perhaps for years. Having a positive outlook can help you make a breakthrough, or turn the corner, if you will, to take steps toward realizing new or even long-held dreams and goals. You can establish a new way of thinking and new habits if you're serious about it and apply yourself. It takes just 21 days to change a habit or develop a new one. Winning habits serve you and support your success. Losing habits detract from your success.

Toss Out Negative Thoughts and Habits!

If you need to change a habit of negative thinking into positive thinking, practice thinking only positive thoughts for 21 days. Don't allow a negative thought to creep into your conscious mind; evict any that threaten to do so. Also, don't utter a negative word or phrase; reject and retract anything that sneaks into your mind and replace it with an optimistic idea related to your topic of conversation.

If you slip up, you need to start all over again with a new 21 day period. It's wonderful how we can change our habits and attitudes when our desire and commitment is strong enough! Habits and attitudes stem from our mental life. It need only take an instant to change your mind. Change your mind—change your life!

Like anything worthwhile, such a change requires effort. Even though you may truly want to make the change, it's likely you'll still need to work diligently to make it happen. For example, as most successful people have done to reduce the negative input into their minds, you may decide to stop watching

TV, reading the newspaper, and listening to the radio. You could replace these habits by reading positive books, and listening to continuing education tapes—to keep yourself motivated and get more educated in your field.

When you do these things, you are helping yourself shift to a new set of experiences and habits. By surrounding yourself with other forward-thinking individuals, you are increasing the positive input into your mind. This helps you to gather momentum as you pursue your dreams and goals.

You need to patiently persevere as you transform from whatever old habits may have been holding you back, to new habits that'll keep you moving on. After a period of practicing your new habits, you will see, hear, and feel changes taking place within you and notice them reflected in your life. You're letting go of the old and embracing the new. It's likely a period of time will pass before you'll begin to notice and enjoy the positive results of the changes you are making.

So hang in there and keep going. You'll eventually realize your goals and dreams when you persist day by day with a positive attitude. You'll stay on track, doing what you need to do to reach the targets you've set for yourself.

There are people who have negative thinking patterns who don't even realize it—they are so firmly entrenched in the habit. They probably receive sympathy from others, which is what they may think they want. But long-term, the sympathy doesn't help them. It only reinforces their weaknesses—it's a negative emotion. They need people to believe in them, encourage them and support them to use their strengths, so they can pull themselves out of the muck and mire of pity and move on in their life. Perhaps they need to let go of the idea that misery loves company, and embrace the truth that—*success attracts success.*

If certain negative thinking people don't want to change their thinking and insist on dumping on you, they can present an unnecessary challenge you may need to avoid, if possible. However, these people may have a sincere desire to change and they may even tell you so. If so, look at them as they can be, not as they are. Make some recommendations of books and audiotapes that have helped you. Encourage them to make whatever changes are necessary to adopt and maintain a positive attitude so they can move on too. Show them an excellent example so you can become a role model.

The way you think evolves into the way you act or react. If you think negative thoughts, negative results will follow as sure as night follows day. When you think positive thoughts, positive results will follow! But even if the results appear negative at first, you'll discover the benefit in this so-called adversity. You may think change can be challenging, and you're right. You're also right if you think it's impossible—until you change your thinking! *You'll only change when the pain of staying the same is greater than the pain of changing.* You can only move on to a new level by changing the thinking that is keeping you at your current level.

What's Your Focus?

Of course, you need to think about doing something before you do it. How you think about it determines what you'll do. Are you focused on the problem—or the solution? Is your focus positive or negative? Are you looking for the many possibilities, or an excuse to avoid making the change? You can accomplish almost anything you desire—a new job, a promotion, a dream house, excellent health, more time with your family, a thriving business of your own, financial security and freedom, or whatever else you want. However you need to be a possibility thinker and put your mind to the task in a positive manner. You need to keep your focus on positive thoughts—on what you *want* to create in your life, rather than what you don't want. You get what you focus on.

When I was a teenager, my dad told me, "If you think you can do something or if you think you can't do it, you're right." Our thinking is central to our success or lack of it. It's as simple as that.

How Do You Perceive Your Experiences?

You can view events in a positive or negative way as good or bad, depending on how you look at them. You cannot relive your history, of course, but you can choose to have a positive attitude about what happened. How do you normally perceive your experiences? Do you give them a positive or negative spin? Do you often learn something positive as a result of what may appear to be a negative situation or circumstance? Remember the old but true cliches—"There's a silver lining behind every cloud," and "You can't have a rainbow without rain." Look for the good—be a goodfinder!

Here's an example. Would you agree that winning is generally believed to be the ultimate positive event? Did you know that losing, which is usually thought of as a negative event, could actually turn out to have a positive benefit? Losing gives all of us a marvelous opportunity to learn from our mistakes—to discover what *not* to do! That, of course, is the positive side of losing. You strive to win, but as my dad told me years ago— "Regardless of whether you win or lose, it is more meaningful that you always do and be the best you can." You give it your best shot. What more can you do? That's a positive philosophy that can benefit us all.

As we go through the ups and downs of life, we all need to remember that every challenge brings with it an equal or better reward. We just need to look for the benefit and accept it.

Now let's take a look at a situation many regard as misfortune—losing a job. Perhaps someone worked for a company for 20 years. They steadily climbed the ladder of success and reached a leadership position. They are accustomed to a six-figure salary and all the perks—bonuses and the like. All of a sudden, a larger firm comes in and takes over their company. The new firm weeds out the top executives, of which they are one, gives them a severance package, and bids them farewell. How do they perceive this situation?

Are they bitter or better from their experience? Say, after their initial shocked reaction, they remain angry and resentful, bemoaning what happened and how unlucky they are. Their discontent spills over into their personal life and few people who care about them have the courage anymore to ask them how they are. They are applying for as many jobs as they know of—yet they've gotten nowhere. No one seems to be interested in hiring them. All the potential employers breath a sigh of relief when their interview with this person is over, because all they seem to do is complain about their old employer and how unfairly they were treated.

Now, you might say, isn't being negative about a job loss a typical way to react? Yes, it is. But remember, they are the people who don't succeed, aren't they? So are they the ones to duplicate? Only if you want the average results these people are getting from their "Woe is me," negative attitudes! It's easy to blame others for your circumstances and situations, and these negative-thinking people often do just that.

They, perhaps subconsciously (we'll give them the benefit of the doubt!), want to avoid taking responsibility for their role in any particular event they experience that they believe is negative. That way, they may figure at some level they won't have to change. But the trap here is that if they don't change, they'll continue to get the same miserable results or maybe even worse!

So, what could the person who lost their job have done to make the loss a win? First of all, it's normal, especially in the beginning, to react negatively if you receive news of a new challenge—it may catch you off-guard. The more personally developed you are, though, the more quickly you can change your attitude and start looking for the benefit in the so-called adversity.

Eventually, you can automatically look for the good, and skip the downward spiral of the initial negativity altogether. This will save you a lot of energy. You'll learn more and more that what happens to you truly happens for your own good, as unapparent as that might seem at the time.

Again, let's take the example of the executive who lost their job. What if they had been truly honest with themselves? Might they have admitted they were at a dead-end in their job—that the real challenges and opportunities were gone? Would they have observed that the firm who was taking over their company had a philosophy that didn't bode well for a good working relationship, even if they had been able to stay on?

Things weren't going as smoothly as they would have preferred. They were just in their familiar, the so-called comfort, zone and hadn't felt motivated to do anything different. However, the loss of their job forced them to face reality. So, grateful in an odd sort of way, that they had the chance to make a positive change. They smilingly put together their resume and set out on the adventure of finding a new opportunity to grow.

In comparison with the negative thinking approach, how do you think the positive thinking approach will be? Would an employer be more inclined to hire someone who's positive or negative? Ironically, no matter how negative the employer may himself or herself be, they'd probably want an optimistic employee!

Is one of your goals to enjoy each day and the wonders of life? Then you need to turn every negative experience into a positive one. Did it provide you with an unexpected chance to make a needed change? Did you learn something from it? Did you meet new people and develop new relationships? If you say yes to any of these questions, that qualifies a challenge as a positive event, doesn't it? It pays you to always be open minded and look for the good in every situation, no matter how it may first appear.

Laughter Is the Best Medicine

Your attitude affects your health. If you have a negative attitude, it adversely impacts your health. In fact, it's been reported that people with a negative attitude have a 19 percent greater chance of premature death! Whereas when your attitude is optimistic, you positively affect your health. Have you noticed that when you're upbeat, you feel more energetic? When you think positive thoughts, which puts a sparkle in your eye and a smile on your face, you think happy thoughts. How could that be anything but good for you?

Laughter comes easily for most. Even so most people don't laugh enough for their own good health. Illness is generally not considered a laughing matter, but perhaps it would help us to poke fun at ourselves if we're not as well as we could be. Laughter is a form of mental jogging. It moves our internal organs, is energizing, stress reducing, life affirming, and helps you deal with challenges. Lightness supports us; heaviness weighs us down—so let's be lighthearted as much as possible.

Is it just coincidence that most comedians live a long life? Consider the longevity of Al Jolson, Jimmy Durante, Bob Hope, George Burns, Red Skelton, and Milton Berle, to name a few. Why is this?

While they make others laugh—they laugh (at least inwardly), and that helps them and other people relax and have fun. Laughter and positive feelings release endorphins into the body. These are proteins that occur naturally in the brain and have potent pain relieving properties that can work wonders to heal an illness. Endorphins are natural painkillers and mood elevators.

Laughter allows us, at least temporarily, to forget our ills and troubles. It increases our pulse rate and gives our respiratory system a good workout.

In his book *Anatomy of an Illness*, Norman Cousins relates that he had a serious and life-threatening disease. His prognosis was poor. Knowing that, he realized his only hope for recovery lay within himself. He was convinced that, along with his doctor's guidance, a cheerful, fun loving attitude, hope, and faith would help him recover.

He would not allow a negative statement or thought to invade his conscious mind. He rented a motel room, borrowed a movie projector, and viewed old Marx Brothers comedies and *Candid Camera* TV shows to help him laugh and feel happy. Endorphins were released and, to the amazement of his doctors, his disease went into remission. Cousins lived many more productive years and continued his research on how our state of mind affects our bodies.

When you are well, laughter can help you stay well; if you aren't well, it can help you get well. It has a curative effect on emotions, body, and mind. It's contagious, allowing your family, friends, and associates to catch it, helping them fight their health and emotional problems as well. Laughter can be used daily as a delightful cost-free therapy.

Keep your life fun as much as possible. Learn to laugh easily and don't take yourself too seriously. A lot of the things you may be worried about, in the long run, probably don't really matter. You're not alone—we *all* need to remember this! So do your best to put things into perspective. It'll help you be healthier and happier. Ask yourself, "Will this matter in five years?" Oftentimes, situations are not worthy of thought—even *next week*—let alone in five years!

We can, with practice, become better and better at taking the challenges of life in stride. We can learn not to over analyze them and better control our attitude and emotional response. As a result, we'll have more energy to work through the situation, others will enjoy being around us more, and we'll be happier and more successful. It's definitely worth the effort!

Is Watching TV Negatively Affecting Your Attitude?

Television is a wonderful invention, but we need to be wary of many of the shows and what we're putting into our mind and the minds of our children. Some TV shows are positive and educational. But many others have inappropriate language, violence, sensationalism, sexual innuendo, and otherwise negative programming.

Talk shows seem to be very popular and draw enormous audiences, but again, beware. Some shows have value and make a positive contribution, but many others have a negative impact and degrade rather than enhance individual values with ineffective role models. TV's predominance of negative stories, often with only an occasional flicker of someone making a positive difference, only serves to discourage and scare people, rather than instill hope and encourage them.

The content of the average TV show undermines rather than supports your success. It's meant to entertain and distract people from the dullness of their everyday lives. Most people dislike their work, and rather than do something productive about it, they look for a mental escape through the media hype and melodrama. They live vicariously through others who, in many cases, are being paid big money to perform.

The sensationalism often displayed by this type of entertainment is, if the ratings are an indicator, loved by a large segment of society, even though the topics often have a negative connotation—playing on the misfortunes of others.

The majority of viewers who seem to always have the drone of the TV as the most constant presence in their home are unsuccessful and unhappy. They have a habit of passively passing their time, often several hours a day, on such potentially harmful shows. They may be momentarily escaping their boredom and dissatisfaction.   But they're just trading short-term pleasure for long term pain as they absorb their daily dose of negativity.

Plain and simple, there seems to be very little on TV to enhance your life. Are you serious about your goals and dreams? Then invest your time wisely. Instead of just allowing TV to lull us into passivity and perhaps negativity, if that's what we're doing, we need to dedicate that time to working toward our dreams and goals.

We need to be living our life—rather than watching others on TV—many who are portraying losing ways. This is one secret to success that seems to escape many people who, day after day, use the 24 hours we're all given in nonproductive ways. They fail to realize that time use is mostly habits. Such people keep doing the same thing—whiling away their time, often meaninglessly and sometimes with the purpose of passing time. Then they wonder why they aren't successful!

If we're failing in life, it's up to us to make the necessary changes in our attitudes and habits in order to win. Life is a do it to yourself project and we may be hindering our own success without even realizing it. When we want better results, we need to adjust our attitude and create new habits that become second nature, to do whatever it takes to get those results.

To lead an uncommonly successful life, we need to do uncommon things! Certain people are successful because they do things others aren't willing to do. For some of us, that includes turning the tube (TV) off and activating ourselves to take action toward our dreams. We need to keep our attitudes positive and establish new habits that support us in achieving our goals.

How Laughter and Attitude Helped Me

Let's talk some more about how important laughing and a positive attitude can be to your well being. A positive, lighthearted attitude, especially toward illness and disease, is one of the most powerful forces in the world. My personal belief in and practice of a positive attitude and laughter was put to a rigid test three-and-a-half months after I retired, when I was recuperating from a near-fatal heart attack.

As I laid in the emergency room, without full knowledge of the seriousness of my illness, I said to myself, "Why me?" After a few minutes I gathered my thoughts, let go of the victim mentality, and started taking responsibility for whatever I may have done to cause the attack. I said, "Why not me?" I vowed at that moment that I would beat whatever challenges I had. I decided to be better—rather than bitter.

I maintained a positive attitude and watched comedies during the four weeks I was hospitalized in the cardiac unit. I managed to boost my attitude, but I still didn't understand my illness because of the lack of any previous health problems!

A complete physical, including an EKG (Electrocardiogram) six months prior to my illness, showed me to be in excellent physical condition. I had been exercising regularly for 25 years; my diet was reasonably good; I didn't smoke; and my blood pressure had always been favorable at 120 over 70.

I had all the appearances of being at very low risk for a heart attack—except for *one* thing many people may gloss over as insignificant. I had been under a great deal of negative *stress*, as I describe in the next chapter.

Stress is now recognized as an important cause of coronary heart disease. As such it needs to be considered as a major risk factor for heart disease and other illnesses, both mental and physical.

My nurses and doctors were surprised and pleased with my attitude and progress—especially after I went into cardiac arrest only a week after the attack. My wife Debby, and our daughters, Judy and Kathy, who had grown up with a positive and happy attitude, maintained their optimism. Their prayers and support made it easier for me to remain on *the positive road of recovery*— which could be likened to the road of success and recovery from financial challenges!

I joked with the nurse who woke me up every two hours for a blood pressure check, the one who gave me a pill at four a.m., and the technician who drew two vials of blood each morning at five-thirty. When they asked, "How are you?" I always responded, "Wonderful," or "Terrific!" (Remember, focus on what you want.)

Debby told me only the positive and happy events of each day, and she was incredible at concealing her concern. Judy, Kathy, and my grandchildren were always upbeat when they visited, and I received many humorous cards and notes from friends, family, and business associates.

I was flown by helicopter from the small local hospital, where I was originally admitted, to the United State's University of Pennsylvania Hospital in Philadelphia. More sophisticated tests were available there. On the way, I joked with the pilot and the paramedics, who were probably also astonished at my enthusiastic, fun-loving state of mind!

Even though I had substantial heart damage, I continued to amaze the medical staff with my recovery. My strong will to live, a positive, happy attitude, and my belief pulled me through this traumatic ordeal.

I truly realized that—*if it is to be, it's up to me!*

The Power of Positive Attitudes

A few years ago, Norman Cousins wrote an article that really impacted me. It was titled *Hope Can Make You Well*, and it appeared in the *Parade* magazine section of our Sunday newspaper. Segments of this article are reprinted here with permission from *Parade*, and Mrs. Norman Cousins, as follows:

"The surgeon had actually seen the malignancy and couldn't get at it with his knife. He gave the young man a week, ten days at the most to live. He knew the nature of the cancer and its propensity to spread. Yet, after six years had gone by, something had kept it from spreading. What was the cause?

This question has relevance not just for this young man, now twenty-four, but also for the thousands of cancer patients who have outlived the melancholy forecasts of the specialists. What most of these survivors have in common is their *attitude* toward their illness. These patients didn't dispute the diagnosis; they just defied the death verdict that went with it.

Why does a blazing determination to live make a difference? A new branch of medicine, Psychoneuroimmunology, which deals with the interactions between the brain, its endocrine system and the immune system, is producing some answers.

Intense determination and hope, it has been discovered, can have a physiological effect. Positive feelings, studies show, can actually stimulate the spleen, producing an increase in red blood cells and a corresponding increase in the number of cancer fighting cells. These cells can destroy the cancer cells one by one leaving normal tissue untouched. This is not like chemotherapy, which cannot distinguish between normal and malignant cells.

That particular emotions can affect our bodies has been supported by various research projects. Harvard Medical School students were tested for immunoglobulins, which are a good index to the immune function, before and after viewing an amusing film. There was a measurable increase in the immunoglobulins after laughter.

Such research is making obsolete the scientific notion that the central nervous system and the systems that control the immune and endocrine function are separate. All the positive forces—love, hope, faith, will to live, determination, purpose, festivity, and laughter—are powerful antagonists of depression. They help to create an environment that makes medical care more effective. It's nonsense to debate the usefulness of the body's healing forces versus the forces of medical science. In illness you want to mobilize all the help you can get. The body's own healing system coupled with appropriate treatment can, between the body's own healing system and the medical one, support one another when given half a chance.

The ability of the human body to turn back illness is one of the wonders of the world. Indeed, the more we know about the connection between mind and body, the greater the prospect that we can put it to work for our greater good."

Negative Thinking Can Make You Sick

Not only can negative thinking stop your success, but it can actually make you sick. It has become more and more widely understood and accepted that there is a mental/emotional factor in almost every physical disorder. In fact, it's estimated that from 50 to 75 percent of people who visit doctors are suffering from a mental/emotional caused illness. Anxiety, fear, and distress—all negative emotions—can, without question, affect your health.

Some people are more predisposed, perhaps through family behavioral patterns or hereditary factors, to respond physically in certain ways to the challenges of life. For example, a person may have a family history of responding to stress by internalizing it and developing stomach ulcers.

The great news is that we can all unlearn unhealthy thinking patterns that may have been passed on to us unintentionally from one generation to another. We don't need to stay stuck in a negative mental state. We can learn how to cope more effectively with situations in our life.

Virtually nothing that happens to us is either inherently good or bad; it's our thinking that makes it so. Whenever you need to overcome a challenge to achieve your goal or dream, it's a golden opportunity for you to grow and move up on your ladder of success.

Did you ever hear someone say, "I'm sick and tired of my job"? Have you ever felt that way? Some people get sick at the very thought of going into work. Amazingly, 70 percent of people in the U.S. don't like their work. Perhaps they need a change of some sort. They may need to transfer to another position that they would enjoy, within their company. Maybe they can trade duties with a coworker. They may be bored and looking for a new challenge. Some people simply need to change careers. Others may be happier if they could work from home, either for their employer as an independent contractor, or in their own business of another kind. The best scenario is to be doing something you really enjoy, wherever or whatever that may be. It can help you stay positive and healthy!

Some people actually imagine themselves to be sick and suffer all the pain and anguish of the real thing, even though there is nothing physically wrong. That's the most extreme end of the spectrum.

More Tips

How else can we avoid or rid ourselves of negative thinking? Here are a few suggestions that can help you:

♦ Think positive thoughts and do not imagine something is wrong. If you catch yourself focusing on the negative, stop yourself and say, "I'm letting go of all negative thinking," and proceed to focus on the positive. Be a goodfinder!

♦ All work and no play isn't healthy. Say you're working full-time, have a busy family, and even a business on the side. You may not think you have time for fun. Learn to blend fun with your job or your business.

For example, say you have an out-of-town job or business trip coming up in Orlando, Florida. Perhaps you can take your family along. You may want to take off an additional day or two to go to Disney World or to see some of the other tourist sites that interest you (of course, if it's financially wise for you to do so).

Take some of your sales staff or business associates and go dreambuilding and meet some new people while you're doing so. Look at some beautiful properties or visit a car, boat, or builders show, or some other dream-reinforcing activity. You'll be getting to know your salespeople or associates better as well as building your dreams and theirs, and meeting new people at the same time. Take pictures and laugh a lot.

Some activities you now enjoy may need to be put on hold when you're chasing after a big goal and investing more of your time in that direction. You can still have a lot of fun with the process of making your goals and dreams come true—and it'll help you maintain a positive attitude.

♦ Remember there are certain things you can't change. Don't fret over them. Instead accept what you can't change and devote your energy to those things you *can* change. Do it with a positive attitude, letting go of any negative attitudes—looking for the good in the situation, and moving on.

♦ Put humor into your life by reading funny books or stories that teach you something too. Also, tell funny stories about mistakes you've made and encourage others to share such stories about themselves. Laugh, especially at yourself, at every opportunity. Have fun as you go about each day. Look for the humor in everyday events and you'll find it more and more easily, as time goes on.

♦ Be grateful for what you have. Gratitude is a sure antidote for an ailing attitude. For example, if someone does something you don't like—displaying unskillful behavior—make a list of all the positive things they do. As your heart fills with gratitude, amazingly enough, it'll be easier to talk to them about your feelings concerning their behavior and forgive them. Gratitude is a key to happiness and joy—a simple, yet powerful lesson we all need to remember!

♦ Check with your family physician about exercising regularly—enough to raise your heart rate. It produces a natural high and helps to relieve the distress and fear caused by negative thoughts. Combine your exercise with your daily routine and business activities. For example, at lunch you could listen to a motivational continuing education tape on your portable cassette player with earphones on, as you take a brisk walk.

♦ Accept responsibility for your actions—don't blame others for your challenges. Always look to yourself and ask, "What have I done to cause my situation? How can I overcome it?" Your life is in *your* hands. If you're going to move on, you need to be the captain of your ship and steer it in the direction of your dreams and goals.

♦ You need to make decisions that affect your life. Don't delegate those decisions to other people. Gather all the facts you need, consider them carefully, and make an informed decision. Check with your mentor or leader for serious decisions affecting your job or business. Make the best decision you can, then don't worry about it.

Do the best you can to make your decision work. Few things are unchangeable—you may need to alter your course of action in the future. Be flexible and take it all in stride and put it in perspective in terms of its importance in light of everything else in your life. Take action and keep moving. Life is a process.

- Negatives will creep into your life. Recognize them, learn from them, and look for the positives.
- Learn to love yourself unconditionally, i.e., regardless of what mistakes you make and what weaknesses you need to work on. This is the foundation for loving others unconditionally. Do your best to love others unconditionally as well—observing their behavior—skilled or unskilled. Care about them, no matter what they do.

  You may need to love some people from a distance because associating with them tends to be a negative experience. That's okay. You can send them a card occasionally, wish them the best, and even pray for them, if you are so inclined. Love is one of the strongest emotions, and certainly the most positive. Without a doubt the world needs more of it, and it starts when we choose to be loving rather than make a situation more challenging by indulging in the opposite of love.

  Care about others, encourage them to follow their dreams, and create win-win situations in all areas of their life.

- Look for the good you do in your work. It's important that work be a pleasant experience as much as possible. If you find nothing good in what you do or you're not happy doing it, it may be time for change. What is it that you love to do and how can you make money doing it? Or you may be setting yourself up financially so you can have more time and money to do what you love to do. For example, you may be a physician who would love to offer your services for free to the poor in your community or abroad.

  The real key to knowing what you love to do is to ask yourself, "What would I do, even if I didn't get paid?" Remember this—insanity could be defined as doing the same thing over and over while expecting a different result! There's no doubt about it. It takes courage to do something different, but it's worth the effort.

Since your body is affected by negative thinking—be positive! Keep your mind on cheerful and happy thoughts as much as you possibly can—again, be a goodfinder. As King Solomon once said, "Being cheerful keeps you healthy." So, instead of being negative, use your energy to focus and work toward your dreams! You'll be happier and your body will thank you for it!

Your Thoughts Determine Your Life

Noted American psychologist William James once said, "The greatest discovery of my generation is that human beings can alter their lives by altering their attitudes of mind."

You shape your own life, which is determined to a great extent by your attitude. And fortunately it's something you *can* control. When you control and direct your attitude so it's solution-oriented rather than obstacle-orientated, you're taking charge of yourself. This will give you greater power over what actually happens. You won't be at the mercy of being buffeted around by the challenge of rising above your circumstances. It'll be easier to respond thoughtfully, rather than over react because of feeling out of control.

You think, feel, and act toward yourself and others as you do often because of unsolicited comments you heard from your parents, teachers, religious sources, and in fact, anyone in authority. When you accept these comments uncritically as necessary feedback about your behavior and act upon what you learn, you're in control of your attitudes and can benefit greatly in the process. This takes a measure of maturity we can all aspire to!

Sometimes, however, such comments produce results that are unwanted, confusing or harmful. This may be especially true if you were very young and/or had little confidence at the time you heard them. You can do nothing about the state of mind you were in at that time. You have the opportunity now, though, to sort out those comments that are valuable to you that support you in winning. If it serves no purpose, let it go. Remember, however, that any comment made to you that you respond to defensively probably has at least a grain of truth in it!

Carefully observe and analyze your attitudes. Are they beneficial or detrimental to your success and happiness? Then, perhaps for the first time, consciously choose to accept or reject them, based on whether they are helpful to achieving your goals. Be your own best friend—not your own worst enemy, as most people are!

The Twelve Attitude Commandments

Here are twelve Attitude Commandments that you may find beneficial in better understanding positive attitudes:

1. Your altitude in life is determined by your attitude, not by your aptitude.
2. The purpose of your existence is not to make a living, but to make a life by making valuable contributions of what you have to give. For example, through your job or business you can make a positive difference in the lives of others, and in yours too.
3. A negative thought is a down payment on an obligation to fail.
4. It may be that you seldom regret anything you've done. But, it's what you *don't do* that you may torment yourself about. Your power to take action is only in the present. You probably know what you need to do to reach your goals. Ask yourself, "If not now, then when?" When will you do what's necessary to make your dreams come true?
5. Never complain. Complaining is the refuge of those who have developed no self-reliance. They assume the stance of a victim and look outward to blame others or circumstances—rather than take charge of their life, as they could. Only those people who have the attitude of self-responsibility turn their wishes into dreams, their dreams into goals, and their goals into reality. These people know that relying on others to make them successful simply doesn't work.
6. The ultimate cost of something is the amount of life you exchange for it.
7. Youth is a state of mind, not a time of life. Wrinkles test the skin, but never touch the soul.
8. People who have not determined their purpose in life are easy prey for anxiety. They're like a ship without a rudder—subject to the force and direction of the wind and waves—bouncing thither and yon.

9. Be enthusiastic. The worst bankruptcy is the person who has lost their enthusiasm.

10. It's not the nature of any particular situation that matters. It's your response to the situation.

11. "Most of the shadows in life are caused by standing in one's own sunshine."—Ralph Waldo Emerson.

12. No one can give you an inferiority complex without your permission. It's a byproduct of your attitude about yourself. So be positive!

You Are What You Believe

Let me share an example with you. One of my former clients, a married woman in her forties who was slim and fit, lost a considerable amount of weight. This caused her to be too thin and aged her twenty years over a relatively short period of time. This was caused by her distress about her health. She felt a lump in her breast and believed she had cancer—even though she had not been to a doctor to either confirm or eliminate her suspicions.

After several months she went to a doctor who, to her surprise, gave her wonderful news. The cyst causing the lump was benign. It was removed with the immediate result that she felt her life revitalized. She soon returned to her normal healthy weight and recovered her youthful looks. Yes, *you are what you believe.*

Fear and anxiety cause stress that can have a debilitating effect on your body and mind. Replace them with the ingredients of a positive attitude—including such virtues as faith, belief, responsibility, trust, common sense, compassion, diplomacy, open-mindedness, unselfish giving, courage, self-motivation, gratitude, integrity, and hope.

Remember, if it is to be, i.e., if you're going to have and maintain the attitudes of a person who wins, it is truly up to you. No one can inject these attitudes into you like a positive-thinking vaccine. You need to sincerely want to win and take appropriate action. That includes associating with and duplicating excellent leaders who have adopted such attitudes into the fabric of their lives.

Chapter Two

How Do You Allow Stress To Affect Your Attitude?

"The harder the challenge, the more glorious the triumph. What we obtain too cheaply, we esteem too lightly; 'tis dearness only that gives everything its value."
Thomas Payne

What Are Your Feelings?

The dictionary defines stress as—pressure, strain, a force that tends to distort a body; intense effort; a factor that induces bodily or mental tension; also a state induced by such stress.

You develop your attitudes and feelings based on your past experiences, your perception of those experiences, what you have learned from them, and your perception of reality in general.

- ♦ Positive feelings include love, gratitude, forgiveness, trust, respect, admiration, and so forth.
- ♦ Negative feelings include distrust, anger, jealousy, resentment, fear, and the like.
- ♦ Indifferent feelings reflect an "I don't care" attitude of ambivalence, i.e., noncommittal "straddling the fence."

Which of these feelings do you hold within you? The most influential factor governing your behavior is how you feel—

which arises from your thinking—i.e., your attitude. Your peace of mind or anxieties, security or insecurity, fulfillment or frustration, success or failure, happiness or sadness all stem from your attitudes and feelings. Understanding these feelings and attitudes are key in preparing you to control stress.

It's impossible to totally avoid having stress in your life. For example, you experience it whenever you do something you don't enjoy. This could include driving in heavy traffic— especially to go to a job you dislike—arriving late for an appointment, working with negative thinking people, and having financial challenges. You can set up your life to do more of what you enjoy, which is probably one reason you're reading this book.

Creating more of what you want in your life, and thus reducing your stress level in certain areas, is part of the answer. It is also possible and highly recommended that you learn to manage stress. Controlled and managed stress is beneficial, because that's part of what drives you toward your goals! Top notch leaders have the ability to manage stress. Failure to manage and thus reduce your stress, can lead to a negative attitude, loss of self-esteem, difficulty in reaching goals, and poor health.

Do You Have a Particularly Stressful Job?

Stress on the job is common. Some people have extremely tight deadlines to meet, like those who generate one or more daily newspapers. Perhaps they're not given adequate time to do a thorough enough job that meets their standards of excellence.

Others may feel overworked or that they are left pretty much to fend for themselves on the assignments they're given—without proper guidance. They may have bosses who manage by intimidation or fail to recognize the contributions they make. Or they may be unclear about the levels of responsibility. As time goes by and they continue to grow and develop, these things may become even more apparent.

At some point in your career you may have noticed others being promoted to positions for which they're not even close to being ready for. They may have been compliant yes people or friends or relatives of the owner. Or perhaps a newly appointed person was given more responsibility than they are prepared to handle. These and many other things can contribute to stress on the job.

A friend of mine is a prime example of someone who experienced stress at work. He worked for the same company since he was age 19, and was eventually promoted to a job he loved—plant manager. His performance was outstanding because he enjoyed both the work and the association with the people for whom he was responsible. He was then promoted to an executive position where he felt uncomfortable and missed the camaraderie with his former plant associates. He also was required to fly to plants hundreds and thousands of miles away, and he hated it because of his fear of flying. No matter how much more they paid him, it simply wasn't worth it.

He had difficulty coping with his anxiety. He felt he no longer had control over his life. Without realizing what he was doing, he was allowing the dictates of his boss to consume him. The emotional and physical turmoil he suffered took an enormous toll on his body—until he just couldn't take it anymore. At age 49 he suffered a severe heart attack and was forced to retire because of the disability that resulted. He believes, and I agree—stress was the primary cause of his illness.

Is Your Stress Controlled or Uncontrolled?

Stress is not a new phenomenon. It has been around for a long time. However, it has only been since the industrial revolution that doctors and scientists have studied it to learn what effect stress may have on the mind and body. Dr. Robert S. Eliot, author of *Is It Worth Dying For?* believes there is evidence that uncontrolled stress can lead to heart disease and sudden cardiac death. Controlled stress, however, can lead to a more productive and happy life. It can not only prolong your life, but also make it healthier and more significant. What kind of stress are you under? Controlled or uncontrolled?

The medical community recognizes six risk factors that are directly responsible for heart disease:

+ High blood pressure
+ Overweight
+ Diabetes
+ Smoking
+ High cholesterol
+ Family history

Stress needs to be added to this list! More physicians now realize that stress can have an adverse affect on our hearts. However, there are still many doctors who, in spite of enormous amounts of research and writings on stress and its negative affects, do not accept this premise.

Of the six—actually seven—risk factors, the only one you can't control is family history. All the other factors, including stress, can be controlled when you decide it is imperative to your health, both mental and physical. It's important to ask for your doctor's advice and support on this.

Controlled Stress Is Necessary for Success

Stress can be beneficial. Without it, we would all have a boring unchallenged existence! Stress can stimulate you to higher achievement that may afford you a more lavish lifestyle. Notice I didn't say necessarily a more enjoyable lifestyle! Managing stress, however, is essential to maintain a healthy balance in your life.

Stress is neither inherently good or bad—it just is. It all depends on your attitude. And fortunately your attitude is under your direct control. You may need to let go of some misperceptions you may have about stress first though. Then it will be easier to make it work for you rather than against you. Maintain a great attitude. It helps tremendously to always look for the positive aspects of what may, at first, appear to be just a negative situation with no benefit. Adversity can be our greatest teacher. Remember the wise words of George Bernard Shaw, regarding adversity: "You have learned something that always feels at first as if you had lost something."

Stress can be defined and identified in quite a number of ways because people perceive it differently. A situation can be stressful to one person, while it is challenging and motivating to another!

Self-Esteem Is Necessary for Success

People who handle and manage stress without experiencing its potential ill affects are able to do so largely because of their self-esteem, i.e., they respect themselves, as well as others. They're also in control of themselves, which stems from their self-esteem. You'll notice they tend to accept and like challenges. They're deeply committed to their purpose—what they believe they were born to do—and to helping others in the best way they can. They tend to be the positive change agents of the world.

These people create win-win situations or nothing at all. Win-lose scenarios are simply not an option to them. They've learned to take themselves lightly, their responsibilities as a contributing member of society seriously, and often consider the process a creative game. They have established a track record of hurdling over countless obstacles and have learned to take the challenges in stride without giving them negative energy, as is the tendency for the average-thinking person.

One such person, commenting about dealing with a person with a demanding, overbearing attitude said, "They can't rattle my cage (upset my peace of mind) because I don't have a cage to rattle." He had just gotten off the phone with a negative thinking, complaining person, who had threatened, in the beginning of the conversation, "I'm going to ruin your day!" To which the recipient replied, "No you're not. I'm not giving you permission!" A person with self-esteem knows that they are in charge of their own attitude.

Low self-esteem is a serious source of stress. It's the root cause of the inability of countless people to handle stress effectively. How come? In many cases, these people don't have the courage to speak up for themselves. So they allow themselves to be "doormats" who are taken unfair advantage of. People can only take unfair advantage of us if we let them. The more we let them, the more stress we experience.

Identifying the Signs of Damaged Self-Esteem

How do you know you or someone else has damaged self-esteem? It is often characterized by a lack of self-confidence, anxiety, anger, resentment and people-pleasing tendencies. Many researchers believe that self-esteem begins with your family environment and is a product of your life's experiences and your responses to them. It can be high or low, depending on your exposure to positive or negative thinking people, and the influence you allow them to have on you, often without fully realizing it.

Some people are raised in an extremely negative thinking environment. They're constantly being put down and ridiculed by people who are important to them (and who supposedly love them). However, there may be one ray of hope in their life—perhaps an interested, supportive teacher or someone else who believes in them and encourages them to do something great. This person keeps rallying for this child to succeed and never gives up on them.

After the child graduates from high school (which the supportive person encouraged them to do), they keep in touch with that caring person, who continues to mentor them and focus on their dreams and positive qualities. The child, now a young adult, may be granted a scholarship to go to the state college where, hopefully, the young person finds another positive thinking individual who helps them continue to rebuild their self-esteem. Or they may be able to be mentored long-distance by their original supporter.

You may be thinking that once a person's self-esteem is beat up, it's gone forever. This isn't necessarily true. It's only gone if they never find an unconditionally caring mentor who helps them rise up from the ashes of the negativity of their upbringing. But anyone who's earnest enough and asks enough people *can* find such a person. That's the main key to regaining self-esteem. It's finding someone who can see past any insecurities and unskillful behavior you may have—to recognize your strengths and to help you repair your self-esteem—if that's what you need and desire to do.

So how is your self-esteem? How do you feel about yourself? Hint—this is reflected in how you behave toward others. Are you quick to find fault? Do you criticize easily? Do you have difficulty showing love and affection? If you have any of these weaknesses as you interact with others, take notice that this is also how you treat yourself. It all starts with you.

Genuine self-esteem is based on humility and an unconditional acceptance of your shortcomings, i.e., your unskilled behavior. No one has perfect behavior. (Although we may sometimes like to think we do!) People with self-esteem always accept full responsibility for their actions.

Do you need to change detrimental habits and behaviors so you can more easily respect yourself? I've never met a person without some habits that could use an overhaul, just in case you think you're alone!

Start by writing a list of things you would like to change. Pick out the highest priority item that holds you back the most from achieving your goals, and work toward changing that behavior first. Sure it will be challenging. But it's necessary to make a change if what you're currently doing isn't giving you the results you want.

So do you have a mentor? Someone who believes in you and is guiding you to help you have and maintain your self-esteem? Is there a leader in your industry who you relate to? Perhaps you and they have a similar educational background? Is there someone who could give you unconditional support as you grow and become stronger in your self-esteem? Is there a leader, perhaps in your organization, who you could counsel with to learn more about becoming a leader yourself and assisting others along the line to pursue their dreams?

Picture yourself as a strong, compassionate leader, firmly grounded in your self-esteem and able to deal with stress easily. There are people like that—and you can be one of them. They had to change their thinking and behaviors in certain areas to change their life, like we all do. Then we can go on to support others in doing the same thing. There's a tremendous amount of joy in helping others. And the more people you help, the more joy you'll experience.

Your life can be more fulfilling and enjoyable. This is true, no matter how developed you are! You always have more potential than you realize. As each new behavior you adopt becomes a habit, go back to the list and choose additional behaviors to change. Ask for help from your mentor. When you're finished with your first list, make out a new one and keep going. Keep growing and becoming the best you can be every day of your life. As former U. S. President Theodore Roosevelt once said, "Do what you can with what you have, where you are."

Here's a contemporary version of an excerpt from *The Autobiography Of Benjamin Franklin* where Franklin talks about his approach to changing his behaviors. This idea can help you make the necessary changes to build your self-esteem and deal effectively with stress. Take it step-by-step, like Franklin did, and you'll find it more easily doable:

> *"I intend to adopt all of these virtues— temperance, silence, order, resolution, frugality, industry, sincerity, justice, moderation, cleanliness, tranquility, chastity, and humility. However, I decided that I would not strive to acquire all these qualities at one time. As I master each one, I'll go on to master the next quality etc, until I have developed all thirteen... "*

Positive Thinking Can Help You Live Longer

Endorphins, as we discussed, are triggered by exercising at an increased heart rate. Known as a natural healer, endorphins are produced by the brain through having a positive attitude and laughing.

On the opposite end of the spectrum, catecholamines, chemicals released throughout the body by excessive stress, can damage blood vessels and arteries. It may take years before the damage is severe enough to affect your health.

However, your arteries and heart can only take so much abuse before they react and cause serious coronary damage. A sudden stressful situation can trigger an immediate realization that something is wrong.

Anyone exposed to and thus programmed with negative thoughts, in most cases, is a prime target for stress related problems. Fortunately, having goals and dreams you're working toward, a positive attitude, enthusiasm, hope, belief, associating with other positive thinking people, intact self-esteem, confidence, determination, and high expectations can be a deterrent to these problems.

Also key to shifting from negative to positive thinking, thus reducing stress levels, is to be on a continuing education program of positive books, tapes, and seminars. Such a program can help you reprogram your thinking to eliminate and replace negative ideas with positive ones.

This can be as simple as reading a personal development book rather than a mystery, listening to a motivational tape rather than rock music and the negative news on the radio, and attending a productive seminar instead of going to a violent movie. Again, it's all about changing habits.

Dr. Eliot indicates research has shown that people with positive thoughts live longer than those with negative thoughts. Positive ideas fill you with positive energy and anticipation. Whereas, negative ones drain and discourage you. It's pretty easy to believe in the power of the positive to enhance your physical and mental well being, isn't it? After all, the evidence of its benefits are now recognized by the medical community.

What Causes Stress?

The underlying cause of stress is usually the belief that we're not in control of our life, i.e., of ourselves. We may perceive ourselves as a victim of our circumstances to one degree or another. The amount of stress we experience generally relates to the amount of control over our life we have "lost," i.e., given to others.

For example, those people who are at the bottom of an organizational structure, perhaps in a secretarial role, can be the most stressed out. They usually have very little formal control and many demands are made of them. It may seem more stressful to be in a management or executive role because of the greater responsibility and decision making that the jobs entail. But ironically, those people, because they have more control of their life on the job, are likely to be less stressed. Of course, there are always exceptions to this—but this is often the case.

Stress is sometimes caused by the perception of a threat, either physical or emotional. It could be fear of losing a job, of not being able to pay all the bills, or concern about something else.

Part and parcel of the fear comes from the concern that whatever happens, we may not be able to handle it. Developing the faith and confidence that, perhaps with help, we can handle anything we're faced with is the main stress eliminator. It behooves all of us to be alert to this and strive to develop this attitude.

What Are the Warning Signs?

Fortunately, there are stress warning signals that tell you when something is wrong. However, these signals are not the same for everyone. Reactions to circumstances differ from person to person because of the influence of their environments, experiences, and attitudes.

Some of the physical warning signals are: frequent indigestion, tightness in the neck or shoulder muscles, frequent headaches, difficulty in sleeping, and a racing heartbeat. Among emotional warning signals are: anxiety, fear, anger, resentment, and distress about what is happening in your life.

We all need to manage stress certainly for our health, but also so we can maintain our self-control and rational behavior. Healthy stress management leads to an even greater sense of control. It can also cause a chain of positive events to occur, which you can think of as a reward for managing your stress! In the process, you may need to learn to identify oncoming stress. This will help you ward against a negative pattern—by interrupting it. Cut it off at the pass, so to speak, with a positive attitude and action. This will be key in helping you gain positive momentum toward handling stress effectively.

How Can You Manage Stress?

You and only you are in control of your emotions and only you can change them. Nobody has that power over you, unless you give it to him or her. And nobody can ruin your day unless you let them! Events happen, and they usually can be interpreted in a number of ways. Through your thinking you filter the event from your own perspective, from past experiences.

Depending on your attitude about the event resulting from your thinking, you'll feel certain emotions. If you interpreted the event to be positive, you'll feel happy. However, if you perceived the event as a negative one, you'll be unhappy. A simple example of this is a rainstorm. If you're a farmer and you have just been through a long drought, you'd be mighty happy to finally see some rain. On the other hand, if you were on vacation and had planned to go swimming in the ocean that day, you'd probably be disappointed, at least at first.

So how do you manage your attitude so that a momentary feeling of disappointment doesn't grow into a daylong negative attitude that would affect you and others? First you would accept the fact that you cannot change the weather and then relax with it—let go of the tension in your body. Then you would look for something else fun to do, perhaps indoors, that you would enjoy as much or maybe even more.

Look for the good in everything and everyone. As Dale Carnegie once put it, "Remember happiness doesn't depend upon who you are or what you have; it depends solely upon what you think."

Go for excellence, but don't expect perfection—from yourself or others. Remember, nobody's behavior is perfect. People with perfectionist attitudes are more prone to stress unless and until they become flexible in their attitudes. Such people need to let go of the idea that their way is the *only* way. They also need to delegate—allow other people to get things done—even though the other person's approach may be different to obtain the same basic result.

Learn to adopt the attitude that you'll go for the results you want with all your heart, but you're unattached to the outcome. You won't let yourself get upset even if the worst thing, in your opinion, that could happen does happen. Know that you can handle it, whatever it is. Whatever the results are, getting all riled up would just make matters worse. That way you will be as prepared as possible for the consequences—without stress. Strive to do your best and you'll often get excellence along the way. And even if you don't, you gave it your best shot. What else can anyone do?

Say you're building your profession or business to gain more freedom and control, but in the meantime you may still have a fair amount of responsibilities to juggle. One technique for managing stress is to list the things you need to accomplish each day or week into two categories.

The *first* category includes things you need to do but don't like to or are afraid to do. Perhaps you've been putting off calling the people on your prospect or potential customer list. Put this in the first category! Even if you're afraid, *do it anyway* and watch what happens! We grow the most when we do the things we fear. And as we do, the fear goes away! The things we are fearful of doing are the things we need to do the most. Have you ever noticed that?

Take the first category and attack that list with gusto and determination to get it out of the way. You may be surprised how easy it is to do those things once you get out of inertia and get going. Getting started is the biggest part. Once you do that, the rest will go—almost naturally. Then go to the second category.

The *second* category consists of things you need to do and like to do. If you do only the things you like to do first, as you may have done in the past, you may experience unnecessary stress. The negative anticipation of later doing what you don't enjoy or are afraid to do may be worse than just getting those tasks out of the way in the first place! You'll be more relaxed, and have less stress—both in the short and long run by first accomplishing those things in category one. While you're doing them, you can look forward to doing the things you like to do as a reward for finishing the category one items! The anticipation of doing something you like to do can be as great a joy sometimes, if not more, than the actual participation!

To manage stress effectively you need to know what's causing it. Write down the things in your life you believe are stressful. Take each item and think what you can do to reduce, eliminate, or change the things that cause you undue stress. Some you can change, perhaps with the help and support from your family and friends, and some you can't change. (You may be surprised how much you really can change when you're committed to doing so.) However, you will be in a better position to make that determination by reviewing the list. Then you can take appropriate action.

Change What You Can

Alcoholics Anonymous uses a familiar prayer to help people sort things out: "God grant me the courage to change the things I can, the serenity to accept the things I cannot change, and the wisdom to know the difference."

For those things you can change, list what and how changes can be made, and then decide when they will be made. Take high stress items first and work down the list. For example, you may have a number of so-called friends who have really been negative toward you since you began seriously building your career or business and following your dream. Perhaps you need to associate with more positive thinking individuals who are also moving on. Put this on your list.

Your goals and dreams need to be central focus points in your quest for a fuller, richer, more satisfying life. You need to be drawn by your dreams and goals to propel you on your journey of success. You need to have some big dreams—some things that may seem impossible without help, to stretch upward as you strive to make them a reality. Many leaders will tell you, especially as they accomplish their dreams, that they challenge themselves to dream even bigger to keep themselves motivated.

Sure you need "impossible" dreams—something grand to go for. However, your goals need to be broken down into workable chunks, so they are realistic and attainable. Goals are, quite simply, dreams with dates on them. If they are impossible to reach within the time frame you set, you'll stress yourself unnecessarily. Your leader or mentor can help you with setting realistic, believable goals.

If necessary, keep resetting your goals until you accomplish them. That's what people who win do—they keep persisting until they *make it happen.* Be ambitious yet realistic as to what you can do, given all the priorities you're probably juggling in your life. You may need to eliminate some less productive activities, at least for now.

Remember though, realistic is whatever you honestly believe! Perhaps you need to raise your level of belief?

Type A Versus Type B Personalities—Which Is Best for Leadership?

Whenever stress is discussed, the term Type A personality often enters into the conversation. What is a Type A and how does it relate to stress? Are there any detrimental consequences to being a Type A? What about a Type B personality? How do they differ?

Drs. Myer Friedman and Ray Rosenman, authors of *Type A Behavior and Your Heart,* were the first to refer to and classify Type A and B personalities. They use Type A to identify those people who have emotional stress, and Type B to describe those who are relatively immune to this stress.

Type A behavior is characterized by an *extreme* sense of urgency, desire for total control, perfectionism, competitiveness, ambitiousness, anxiety, and aggressive, abrasive, alienating behavior.

These folks mostly refer to themselves (i.e., I, me, mine, my) and have huge egos that are out of line; they alienate others. Such people need to learn to be gently assertive or else they'll overwhelm others—like their prospects, customers, clients, and even their own associates, friends, and family!

Type B behavior is laid-back, relaxed, content, peaceful, calm, and assertive rather than aggressive. The result is, they can be more productive than the Type A by sharing with, leading, and supporting others to determine for themselves what the right thing is for them to do, rather than expending energy trying to control others. They know their energy can be better used to build their business or career through an empowering, rather than an intimidating approach. Type B personalities are humble and gracious—knowing, as someone once said, "Teamwork makes the dream work."

Nobody really wants to be around a person with hardcore Type A behavior. Their style attracts and supports weakness in others, whereas the Type B attracts and supports the strength in people. The type A tends to be pushy and dictatorial. Whether they realize it or not, their intensity is stressful to themselves, as well as others. Since they can't get away from themselves, they actually suffer more! If the Type A continues this style of behavior, they could be headed for a heart attack. Unfortunately, for some it takes such a serious life-threatening event to wake them up to what they're doing to themselves and others.

It's important to have a sense of urgency and importance about your business or profession—a sense that time is "marching on" and you don't want your life to go by without having achieved your dreams. You're giving your career or business some priority in the scheme of things—considering it to be an important part of your life.

Yet, rather than being overwrought and nerve-wracked about it, like those with Type A behavior often are, you are or need to be doing this with a calm sense of certainty. You may know how fortunate you are to be in the business or career you're in or working toward. It's likely you're steadfastly, with commitment, doing whatever it takes to realize your dreams. You may have already discovered that life, without working progressively toward dreams and goals, is empty and stressful at best. I doubt that a life of just surviving and getting through your days would be anything but mediocrity and mounting stress for you.

But it's likely you're being strong, yet considerate how you treat yourself and others in the process. Are you regularly meeting new people and encouraging them to achieve their dreams? I believe you'll do your best to listen to their needs and wants (dreams) and honestly, empathetically care about them and their welfare, rather than being pushy.

You've probably learned that Type A pushy behavior is stressful all the way around—with those of us who are displaying such behavior often affected the most negatively. You undoubtedly have learned that some people are often like "wet noodles" that you can gently pull (lead) but not push to success.

Type a Behavior and Your Heart

Dr. Friedman believes, as the result of research and studies, that a major cause of coronary artery and heart disease is a complex of emotional reactions, which he designates as Type A behavior.

In his newest book, co-authored by Diane Ulmer, R.N.,M.S., *Treating Type A Behavior and Your Heart,* he states, "We know now beyond any doubt what we suspected before—that Type A behavior can be treated effectively, that reduction or elimination of this behavior can reduce the incidence of second heart attacks radically, and that Type A behavior can now be regarded, alone among risk factors, as a primary causal agent in the pathogenesis of coronary heart disease."

Anger and Resentment Have No Place in Success

Anger and resentment are not the same feeling—even though they're often mistaken for such. Anger is directed at someone or something. Resentment is generated, i.e., directed at *everyone* and *everything.* As some people would describe it, it's having a "chip on your shoulder." This is defined in *The Dictionary Of Cliches* by James Rogers as, "To be edgy, snappish, ready to fight." It's being antagonistic with a feeling of opposition and resistance to others' thoughts, feelings, and actions.

If you are angry or afraid (which is often part of anger), you may tend to focus on the anger or fear. What you focus on gives it energy—makes it have more of a presence in your life. This can produce harmful results health-wise, because if you have these feelings, your blood pressure and pulse can increase dramatically.

If you feel angry or afraid, the great news is that you can adjust your attitude! You need to take some deep breaths and refocus. Shift your thinking to concentrate on something positive like pleasant sounds. This may include waves gently breaking in the surf, soothing music, or the sounds of nature. This relaxing activity can reduce your blood pressure and slow your pulse rate —thus reducing your stress level.

Be Forgiving

Forgiveness helps you diffuse and eliminate anger and resentment. (To forgive doesn't mean to forget or condone someone else's unskillful behavior.) You forgive for your own well being. In fact, you may or may not choose to, or even be able to, communicate your forgiveness to the other person, especially if they have died. Also, you need to remember in order to forgive.

As Jay Rifenbary says in his book *No Excuse! I'm Doing It...*

"If you stay focused on what someone did or didn't do in the past that negatively affected you, you can lose a lot of precious energy that could be directed toward your dreams and goals. You want to look forward and take action, rather than allow yourself to stay stuck where you are. You may need to loosen up; then let go of the control you've allowed someone else to have over you so you can move on."

Be Appreciative

Another key to adjusting your attitude and letting go of anger and resentment is to *adopt an attitude of appreciation*. For example, it is easier to be positive when you take an honest look at all the good you have in your life, in general, and all the good the person who offended you has done. Write them a letter expressing your thankfulness for what they've done to make a positive difference in your life. You can choose to send it or not. This process helps you to get the challenge in perspective and melt away your anger.

As you've undoubtedly noticed, we're living in a world of people who often have unskilled behavior. All of us need to cope with this reality and know that our behavior isn't always skilled either, as much as we may not want to admit it! In a majority of situations, both parties contributed in some way to the challenge at hand. There may have been a lack of clear communication, which is often the case.

Acknowledge and Accept Responsibility

One of the most effective stress relievers is to *take responsibility* for your part of the situation and readily admit you made a mistake. This often diffuses the situation. Being defensive only escalates the high volume discussion and thwarts resolution of the disagreement.

Beyond taking responsibility for our role in the situation, we need to focus our comments on the *behavior* of the person(s) we're dealing with. Labeling and name-calling will only antagonize them.

For example, later in the process of building their business, an entrepreneur may invite a friend to become a business associate. Their friend then may say, "I feel disappointed that you didn't invite me to join you in your business when you first started it." You could reply, "You said you were so busy as it was—that you wished you could take a vacation and never come back. So I figured you would just say no anyway, so why bother?"

They may respond, "Well, you didn't even give me a chance." You could say, "You're absolutely right. I could've shown you the business plan last year, then you could have enjoyed the growth of the business, like I have. I apologize for my mistake. I'm really sorry." To which they may (hopefully) respond, "I understand. To help make up for it, let me join you now and we can go from here and build it together." This is certainly an example of an interaction with an almost ideal prospective associate. Nonetheless, the point is, we need to address and resolve such issues in a self-controlled, respectful manner.

We all need to work through business and personal challenges, let them go, and move on. Holding on to anger and resentment and not forgiving, claims your valuable energy and keeps you stuck. Peace of mind is attainable as we diligently confess our mistakes, forgive others and ourselves, and persistently endeavor to create win-win situations in all areas of our lives.

You may be feeling angry and resentful toward others who never seem to understand what you're striving to achieve in your career or business. They may have given up on their dreams years ago, referring to them as a joke or as "pie in the sky." They might even be referring to your dreams as farfetched. Deep down inside they're probably jealous.

Let Go of What Negative Thinking People Do

As you move on, you're likely to find that you need to *let go of certain people* in your life, like these individuals who are pulling you down with their negative attitude. This may be uncomfortable, especially at first, but it's all part of developing you and finding people to associate with who are like-minded and positive thinking. You need people who'll encourage you in your quest for financial freedom or whatever it is you are striving for in your business or career. If the opportunity even exists for them to join you and they don't choose to do so right now, they may later.

Impatience Verses Enthusiasm

People with Type A behavior mistake impatience for enthusiasm. They feel super aggressive behavior will bring quicker and increased success. Instead, it slows them down as it makes others less inclined to want to be around them or work with them.

However, people with Type B behavior invariably have greater and longer lasting success. They are just as creative and enjoy more harmonious relationships with their families, associates, leaders, friends, and other people.

You may be saying to yourself, "Oh my gosh, I've been doing Type A things for years." That's okay. All of us, no matter how "together" we may appear to be, have done things that in retrospect, after growing some, we'd certainly do differently. So you're definitely not alone. The good news is, each moment is a new beginning, and we can all change our thinking and behavior to be more like the person we'd like to be. This helps us to go forward and achieve our dreams and goals. We don't need to stay the same—we can move on in whatever areas we want to. It's our choice.

More Ideas to Reduce Stress

Listening to continuing educational and motivational tapes, and reading positive personal growth (i.e., self-help) books, are helpful in unwinding from the day to day activities that tend to be stressful. A dual purpose is served in these activities: you're helping yourself to grow, which then enables you to better help others with what you and they do in your business or profession.

In change there is opportunity, but there may also be stress. All matters are subject to change, and we all need to be flexible in handling change to minimize or eliminate the stress we experience. Sometimes when we adopt a new attitude, we can eliminate the stress altogether. When we do the best we can, with faith that it'll all turn out for the best, and we're unattached to the outcome, our stress can disappear!

Time/activity management, discussed in a following chapter, is another method you can use to cope with stress. You can be confident knowing you have the time to do those things that you personally need to do. Perhaps you can delegate some tasks others can do and still be able to do those things that are not as crucial toward reaching your goal, but still are important to you.

Without effective time/activity management people often "spin their wheels," accomplishing little, if anything at all. They flounder by doing category two—often-unimportant maintenance tasks that have little or no effect on their goal accomplishment. The result is they get backed up on the tasks that are important to achieving their goals. Then they wonder why they're not making progress. Unfortunately, few of them look to themselves as the cause of their lack of success! Instead, they come up with some pretty amazing excuses.

As much as possible, surround yourself with people you like who are positive, upbeat, and ambitious. I can't emphasize this enough. Most everyone needs to earn money, to one degree or another. It's certainly much more enjoyable and less stressful to work with people you like and respect, who are going somewhere.

If you are in a position to hire employees or choose your business associates, you have a golden opportunity to select people with an uplifting attitude. This requires more effort in the beginning, but it can pay big morale dividends later. This is especially crucial for those associates or employees who answer the phone. A pleasant helpful attitude on their part is key. Now this selection process may be out of your direct control; therefore, you need to be flexible in your relationships and learn to see something good in everyone. This approach works everywhere for everyone, personally and professionally. Be a good finder. It'll reduce your stress level.

Associate with other goodfinders at every opportunity. Find people who are enthusiastic about life and the chance they have each day to make a positive difference and have fun in the process. Stay away from people who are always moaning and groaning.

For example, if you are a teacher and all the other teachers seem to do in the teacher's lounge is complain—grab a great personal development book and go someplace else and read it. Remain cordial, but don't hang around these people any more than you have to, as required in your work. If you're tagged as a loner, so be it. It really doesn't matter. Those people are stress-inducers and you don't need or want that, do you? Go for stress-reducing activities and people whenever possible. You just need to look for them!

Leaders Make Decisions—Then Make Them Right

You may need to take an action or make a decision you don't want to. Some are easily made, but often they involve complex situations and are arrived at with anxiety and stress. It is important, therefore, to gather all the facts and make your decision rationally rather than emotionally in order to minimize stress. Once the decision is made, don't worry about it. Just make it turn out right. Then watch the results come in.

You can weigh the pros and cons of a decision, but if it's ultimately not made or is delayed, anxiety and frustration can result, leading to excessive stress. It's to your advantage to become an effective decision-maker to avoid stress.

High-performance leaders are positive decision-makers. They are humble enough to ask their mentor for assistance when necessary. Want-to-be leaders, who avoid making decisions and asking for help, are less likely to rise in their organization.

Several basic steps to take in the decision-making process are:

♦ Be sure you know what the situation is. You may need to talk to more than one person.

♦ Determine the ideal ultimate outcome. What results are you shooting for?

♦ Gather all the facts available and determine possible solutions.

♦ Look carefully at alternatives and consequences and weigh them with pro and con lists.

♦ Make the decision based on your research and consult with your mentor or leader, if necessary.

♦ Implement the final decision.

♦ Don't worry about it. Let your decision have a chance to work out.

♦ Stay committed to the decision and do whatever it takes to make it the right decision. If for some reason, no matter what you do, it isn't working out, go back to the first step.

I have been able to handle stress over the years by not worrying about my decisions. I simply did my best to make the wisest decision and then I relaxed with it.

How Well Do You Use Time and Manage Your Activities?

I also handled stress by working hard and playing hard. I traditionally put in long hours, five days a week; however, weekends and vacations were spent in quality time with my family. I had an ability to shut down my thoughts of work as I left the workplace because I was confident that I had a productive day. I looked forward to the next day's challenges and opportunities. I had a positive attitude and had planned for tomorrow—today.

You may have a second job or business in addition to your primary business or job. So, for a while, as you're improving your financial picture, you may be balancing a lot of activities. That's common for people who are digging themselves out of debt and/or transitioning into a new level of income and lifestyle.

So, to keep your stress as low as possible and open up your time outside your main job or business, you may need to have periodic family meetings and delegate some household chores that you'd normally do to other family members. If you don't have children or they're not old enough to do some of the chores, you may want to hire a neighborhood boy or girl or local handy person to help you out. For instance, many people mow their own lawns. This consumes valuable time that could be used to do something to build your financial future.

We all need to guard our time carefully so we can be productive, not just busy. Oftentimes, we need to place more value on our time so we can keep moving ahead, achieving our goals one by one. Then, five years down the road, we can look back with a sense of accomplishment instead of regretting that we didn't invest our time wisely.

How Can You Reduce Stress Through More Effective Communication?

To minimize stress, and as a leader, in general, it's important to build strong positive relationships. This requires consistent effective communication, which leads us to mutual understanding and appropriate action. Communication is not just talking. It's also nonverbal—your attitude about the people you're interacting with, the way you perceive what's being said, the way you listen and hear, and your eye contact. Communication is also other things like your posture, tone of voice, gestures, and the like.

You communicate best when you do so on other people's level of reception. For example, if you share your expertise, products, services, or something else to a prospective customer or associate who has a stressful executive level corporate position, their level of reception is likely to be a corporate mindset. You need to communicate with them how they can benefit from what you're sharing. How can they resolve some of their challenges and get the results they want by associating with you? This can be done by careful listening and observation concerning their needs, wants, and perhaps, dreams.

Empathy is a powerful form of nonverbal communication. It's understanding another's feelings and actions, which only comes from a heart-to-heart talk. It allows you to understand where the person is coming from and to vicariously experience their thoughts and actions. You are on their wavelength, so to speak. This enables you to respond in a manner that allows open authentic communication to flow between the two of you. You can, therefore, advise and assist effectively because of this accord.

Empathy is a positive emotion, while sympathy is negative. Empathy is like when someone is down in a hole and you throw him or her a rope and help them pull themselves out. You support them in their strength and do whatever it takes to help them be victorious. Sympathy is when you crawl in the hole with them and have a "pity party," supporting their weakness. Empathy is an essential quality of an excellent leader. It's a key ingredient to building strong positive bonds with others.

Another form of nonverbal communication is the use and understanding of *body language.* Your body, i.e., your arms, legs, eyes, and posture, reflect whether you have an open or a closed mind. Folded arms and legs, lack of eye contact, and a rigid posture convey a closed mind and a lack of interest and communication. When you unfold your arms and legs, make constant eye contact, lean forward, and above all, face the person you're conversing with, you're communicating your open-mindedness. Listen intently, keep an open mind, and show a keen interest in what is being said. Ask questions to both better understand what they have said and to learn more beyond that. Communicate well verbally and non-verbally. We'll be talking more about this later on.

Effective communication is assertive as opposed to aggressive. Aggressive communication comes from emotional reactions that can be abrasive and domineering. Assertive communication reflects thoughtful consideration of the situation before talking. As mentioned before, it's good to express your feelings about someone's behavior rather than name-calling. The latter labels people and negatively affects their self-esteem. Aggressive communication actually reinforces the negative behavior, and thus increases the possibility that it will occur again! Assertive communication is relationship building rather than relationship harming. You can still get your point across—with less likelihood of a defensive negative response.

Your ability to communicate is influenced by your personal history and your perception of a situation. If you are fearful, injured, or in conflict and your emotions are out of control, you may tend to be aggressive. As a result, your communication skills are dulled and ineffective. You won't be able to affect a positive change in the relationship. Instead, you may just start a shouting match. This doesn't serve anyone. It may just inflame both parties and escalate the disagreement into verbal warfare!

The self-discipline to cool off first and focus on the behavior in question is needed. This, along with empathy and forgiveness of yourself and others, can lead to mutually beneficial long-term relationships in all areas of your life. Grow and take your relationships to the next level through thoughtful assertive expression of your feelings and ideas.

All Work and No Play...

"All work and no play makes Jack a dull boy," as the old saying goes. But it may also make him a stressed out one too!

You need to be active to maintain a healthy body and mind. If you don't do anything, you'll soon be bored. When you are productive at your job or in your business, you put your heart in it and enjoy the process as much as you can. After all, it's your life we're talking about here. This is not a dress rehearsal!

As mentioned before, you can blend vacation time in with an out of town business trip. Say you're at a convention and you have a free afternoon, perhaps you can find something fun to do in the area that your whole family would enjoy. You may even meet some new people that day who turn out to be future customers or even associates! You could stay an extra couple of days and see the area. Some people have even had business trips abroad and have found it a less expensive way to travel with their family.

I've mentioned that you can do enjoyable dreambuilding stress-reducing activities along with your other career or business building activities. Say your company or organization is having a meeting in a hotel in the next town. On the way you could pick up a couple of your salespeople or associates. You could then drive through a local upscale neighborhood to look at the houses, cruise by the local luxury car dealership, and perhaps have a soda or coffee in the beautiful restaurant in the hotel.

This can be a key ingredient in helping you and your people to fire yourselves up for your dreams. We all need something to go towards—to help us to maximize our productivity. Teach others the idea that—*if it is to be, it's up to me*. Have fun as you go along and build relationships in the process and de-stress.

The Need for Delayed Gratification

You need to be careful you're not going overboard in your recreational activities, though, especially when you're busy building your career or business and are at a developmental stage where it requires more time and effort. Practicing some delayed gratification is key. Perhaps you enjoy and have regularly been participating in a number of sports, coaching, hobbies, or other recreational activities. For example, say you're coaching a soccer team a couple times a week where your son or daughter plays. You may have been doing this type of thing for years. If you have a business-related appointment or event scheduled for that time slot, you may want to have a substitute or assistant coach available to take your coaching role.

Some people stop coaching and many of the other activities they used to participate in so they can free up time to invest in their profession or business. To compensate, they diligently blend as much fun as they can with their normal business activities—to reduce stress, yet stay on track with their goals.

You, of course, need to decide for yourself what's best in the long run for you and your family. When you invest time now in building your career or business, say to reach certain financial goals, you may be doing it to reap the time later so you can be with your family *many more* hours. Or you can golf, fish, bike, boat, fly, hunt, ski, bicycle, bowl, or whatever activities appeal to you, *much more* because you've reached your goals. It truly is a balancing act—freeing up the time, working it out to have as much fun as possible, while devoting the necessary time to pursue your dreams and goals.

Adopt the Attitude of "I Enjoy Life"

Enjoying your everyday tasks, in concert with the building of your business or career, helps you to be lighthearted. Remember to laugh a lot! This approach helps you to reduce the stress, anxiety, and frustration that are harmful to your overall health.

Again, take yourself lightly and what you're doing seriously. Laugh a lot and poke fun at yourself, but not at others. Laughter, as we have discussed before, which often results from a playful attitude, is also a powerful medicine for managing stress. And it's free! Be playful most anywhere you happen to be. You'll notice the difference in how you feel. You're also likely to attract more positive thinking people into your life. So do your best to interject fun into your life on a daily basis—no matter what you're doing. It'll help you have a stress-free attitude.

Are You Happy at Work?

A lot of people are stressed-out because they haven't thoughtfully chosen their work. They may have taken the first decent job they were offered, even though the work didn't interest them at all. Or perhaps their parents expected them to work in a particular field or in the family business. And just to please them, they went in that direction, much to their chagrin. A lack of self-direction gets many people into trouble. They do things for the wrong reasons, rather than what's in their heart to do. They fail to follow their dreams, and as a result, they lead unfulfilling lives of not-so-quiet desperation. They often consider themselves to be stuck, but it's only their thinking that makes it so.

Are you one of these people who considers themselves stuck? If so, remember this. It was *you* who chose what you do for a living. Sure, you may have let someone influence you in the process, but nonetheless, it was and still is *your* choice.

Are you just making a living, or are you designing a rich, fulfilling life? Do you enjoy your work? Or do you believe it's your lot in life and you've got to endure it until you retire? Are your retirement years decades away? Do you have children you want to (or feel you have to) put through college? Are you concerned about medical benefits, or is there some other reason you use to justify not making a change? Remember, as a person with freedom of choice, you have every right to make that decision.

But consider this: if you're miserable, it's highly likely you're negatively affecting many or all of those who associate with you professionally *and* personally, including yourself! You've got to live with *you* every second of every minute of every day. You simply can't get away from you! Have you ever considered that? So…what can you do?

You may be thinking you'd like to make a change. But you may want to point out, "It's easier said than done." No kidding! Most things that are worthwhile require a great deal of effort on your part. It's human nature to want it to be easy, isn't it? You're not alone. We're *all* faced with this reality.

Are You Being Honest with Yourself?

Are you tempted to crawl back into your comfort zone, which is probably better labeled as your familiar zone, because it's probably not all that comfortable anymore? Are you starting to rationalize that your situation really isn't all that bad?

Do you know what rationalizing is? It's telling yourself rational lies! For example, you may have a business that owns you. You might have a lot of personal money tied up in it, yet you haven't been profitable enough to get out of it. Perhaps you've been striving to do so for several years now. To top it off, you may not be making any more (or maybe even less) money than an average wage earner. You could even be working 7 days a week! What rationalization might such busy, struggling entrepreneurs tell themselves? "I'm in too deep to get out now," or "I don't know anything else."

Do you like your job? Have you outgrown it? Are you ready for more responsibility? Have you talked to your mentor or boss about it? Are you less productive because you really don't care anymore? Do you need to change careers—to do something you would enjoy more? Are you just making a living? Or are you making a life? Are you going to follow your heart, i.e., your dream, and do what you know you really, really want and need to do? Or are you basically just complaining—surviving day by day? Do you realize that maintaining status quo isn't possible? If you're endeavoring to maintain status quo, you're actually losing ground. Time is the most precious commodity you have. Are you setting yourself up for regret later?

Did those questions help you get a grip on where you are in terms of your job or business satisfaction? Did you gain some new understanding? If so, what is it? Take a piece of paper and write it down now. You may need to look back over the questions. Or you may be struck with another question that you need to answer.

For example, have you been procrastinating in taking needed action concerning your job or business? If so, ask yourself, "What do I need to be doing next that I've been putting off?" And "When am I going to do it?" This could be something as important as scheduling an appointment to talk with your boss, leader, or mentor to discuss your situation and explore your options. How about it?

Change Your Work or Change Your Attitude

I remember a friend and neighbor who, like many people, hated every hour he spent at work. He could hardly wait until he could retire—even though that day was years away. How stressed he must have felt every day at work. I was often tempted to suggest that he quit his job and find something that gives him hope and satisfaction. He just kept complaining, as most people do, yet not taking any action to remedy his situation.

Many people are very unhappy with their work. They're in their rut so deeply, it's almost like a grave with the ends kicked out! They don't seem to realize that what they're doing, day in day out, is only perpetrating their struggle. In some cases, of course, they are negative thinking people who wouldn't be happy even if someone dropped a million dollars in their lap! Sure as the earth is round, they'd still find *something* to complain about!

In those instances, an overall change of attitude could be the only key they need to unlock the door of a new life. They need to look inside themselves for the root cause of their unhappiness and take action to make the necessary changes. They just may need to become a goodfinder, and appreciate the positives they have in their work life, and in other areas as well. Then, should they choose to, they can launch any changes from their new attitude of gratitude. They'll surely attract more positive thinking people to team up with than if they persist in their negative thinking rut!

There is a 77 year-old man who lives in New York. When he was 70 someone introduced him to personal growth through personal development books. He started reading and it changed his life. He comments now, "I was obnoxious for 70 of my 76 years—until I read that first book. I sometimes slip back into my old ways, but it doesn't last very long! I'm still working on it." What happened is that he learned to change his attitude about people. He learned to care about and respect them—to love them—instead of being intolerant and combative.

He also learned how to turn around what appears to be a negative situation and find the benefit(s) in it. He's learned to be forgiving and has actually gone to people for which he harbored negative feelings and totally forgave them. And I was pleased to hear he had even learned to take better care of his body! So it's never too late to change your attitudes!

Some people just need to change their negative attitude about their business or job. They may do a lot of grumbling about everything. They could start by making a list of all the positive things about their job or business. Do you need to do that?

Others need to get really serious about expanding their business or profession. They may gripe that it's not growing—when the truth is they're just maintaining what they have. They're not building it. They may need to take some leadership seminars, read some personal development books, and listen to some continuing educational audiotapes. They simply cannot grow to a new level of success without increasing their level of understanding first. You cannot solve a challenge at the same level in which it was created. It's likely they need to learn to lead themselves before they can effectively lead others.

Some individuals need to explore a career or business change. This takes courage. But taking it one step at a time helps you to get going so you can gain the momentum to do what's necessary. You may need to make a telephone call, write a letter, or search the Internet. An option, of course, is to refuse to explore the alternatives, and to continue to be unhappy. Doing nothing to better your situation just reinforces any idea that you may be stuck.

In today's economy, people can easily be forced to get unstuck. Their employer may be merged, bought out, or closed down. It's better to be the one initiating the change, rather than be surprised and unprepared for it. Don't you agree? It's much less stressful to take charge and explore the possibilities so you're prepared. In fact it can be downright exciting!

It's one sure way to gain more control over your future—and discover some of the many options there are that you may not even be aware of now! Keep going. Ask questions. Be open-minded.

Continue your search until you feel satisfied that you've done your homework and you're poised to take action, if and when you want or need to do so. Who knows where it could all lead? It's definitely worth doing, especially if you're vulnerable to losing your job.

Here's How Stress Almost Killed Me

I had a significant personal experience with stress and it is still difficult for me to understand why I allowed myself to get into this situation. I classified myself as a person with Type B behavior. However, in reviewing my past activities, while I didn't possess all the characteristics of an Type A personality, I did have one or more Type A traits. As Dr. Friedman said, "If you only possess one Type A trait, you are a Type A and therefore are subject to all its consequences."

I loved my career with the large insurance sales company I mentioned earlier. Although it's true that there was stress in my work, I managed it with a positive attitude. The only pressure to produce was self-imposed, i.e., from within me, and I handled that well for years. However, a stressful situation developed three years before my planned retirement that I didn't manage well at all.

The stress started after I decided to retire somewhat early, at age 60—early for the average employee, anyway. I'm not sure why, but I didn't mention my plans to my employer, associates, peers, friends, or even my mentor. Because of my unwillingness to share my decision with anyone outside my family, I became more and more stressed in my daily activities.

I didn't have the additional support and guidance that I could have experienced had I been more open. A lot of people make this mistake of not revealing their concerns, especially major ones, thinking they can handle it on their own. This can truly be a life-threatening decision, as mine was.

I got so wrapped up in winding down and putting things in order, I failed to see the stress signals I had previously recognized and managed so well. I became irritable when things didn't go as planned, and I felt ever more uncomfortable because I still hadn't shared my plans with anyone.

I finally broke the news to everyone in late November with my last day in the office to be in mid-December. On one hand, I felt good about having had a successful career. Nonetheless, I found it was extremely stressful to say goodbye to so many of my friends and associates.

The Big Attack

Three and one-half months following my retirement, I suffered a near-fatal heart attack. After my initial shock, I asked my doctor, "Why?" He couldn't give me a satisfactory reason. Amazingly, he never even mentioned that stress could have been a factor. In looking back, I now believe it was definitely the culprit.

I had managed it well for over 35 years—or so I thought. Perhaps stress had taken a toll on me little by little and had a cumulative effect.

Whatever the case, my coping skills didn't compensate for the stress I felt during my last year of work. I was unaware of what my stress was doing to me, and it almost cost me my life.

Are You Ignoring Stress Signals?

I had ignored several stress signals that, had I been more aware, would have "put up a red flag." For example, there were times when I was impatient with a customer or associate who was behaving unreasonably. I remember tensing up. As my blood vessels constricted, I became short of breath, and my heart began pumping rapidly. However, my tension melted away after a few moments of relaxation. Unfortunately, I never gave it a second thought. This occurred three or four times during the last few months before my retirement.

In addition to the experiences I just mentioned, right before my illness, I remember becoming short of breath twice. Once, while briskly walking on the cart path of our golf course, I suddenly had difficulty breathing. I didn't think anything of it since as soon as I stopped and rested for a few seconds, the feeling left. Two days later the same thing happened; this time while I was swimming. I ignored these signals since I thought I was in good health and still had excellent stamina and felt energetic.

I mention these stress signals specifically because people all too often overlook the warning signs of serious illness— whatever they may be. My body was telling me something, but I wasn't paying attention. Your body talks to you and it's important to listen. You can then often avoid a greater challenge or catch it before it becomes serious, or even leads to sudden death. If you're having a symptom or symptoms that could be a sign of a health challenge, I suggest you consult with your physician. Ask questions. "You and those you love may be very glad you did.

To further emphasize the need for your alertness to your own body talk and your need to question your physician, I'll share an experience where even my family doctor ignored a warning signal! I had my annual physical two months before my retirement.

My blood pressure was elevated to 160 over 90, while my history showed that before this, it had always been 120 over 60. My doctor advised me to have it checked every day at the same time for ten days. I did this, and it slowly went back to its normal level. This too was a false indicator that I was okay—which I wasn't.

I believe stress was responsible for the increase in my traditionally consistent blood pressure, and this was a signal that could have alerted my physician to this fact. I rationalized this signal because I had too many things on my mind to be concerned, so I didn't take my body's signal seriously. My health is my responsibility and I could have taken steps to determine the cause of the problem. But I failed to do so, and I suffered the consequences, as we all do. Chances are that proper diagnosis and treatment could have reduced the severity of my heart attack, or even eliminated it altogether.

According to Dr. Friedman, few physicians admit to his well-documented facts, proving that stress is a major risk factor in diagnosing heart attack victims. (Perhaps that's because they're so stressed-out themselves!) I was one of the fortunate 50 percent who survive their first attack. I'm grateful that I have a second chance at life, and an opportunity to share some valuable information with you. Hopefully, you won't have to go through the same type of undiagnosed (or diagnosed, for that matter) stress-related illness. Do what you can to avoid it.

Living Healthier

Since my attack, I have taken the recommended steps to live with my damaged heart. I feel as good or better than I have ever felt. I avoid stressful situations, and I take events in stride. I don't worry about the things I can't control.

I have also changed my lifestyle. I maintain a diet of low fat, low cholesterol food, vitamins and supplements, and regular exercise has helped me recover both mentally and physically.

Stress can be as silent a killer as hypertension. Therefore, we all need to develop a positive plan to manage and control our stress so its potentially devastating effects can be minimized or even eliminated altogether. And, most important of all, your plan needs to include having a positive mental attitude. To get positive results, you need to first have a positive attitude.

Are You Enrolled in a Continuing Education Program?

More and more cutting edge organizations, corporations, and other entities are becoming aware of the value of having an ongoing continuing education program of monthly books and tapes, as well as, in many cases, monthly seminars and training sessions. Perhaps you're reading this book as a part of such a program. It could be key not only to your success in your career or business and in your personal life, but also less obviously to your physical and mental well being.

People all over the world have been at the bottom and have enriched their lives in so many ways by plugging into a continuing education program often offered to them by their employers, leaders, or mentors. I personally know some of these people. Their development into fulfilled, contributing members of society has been directly related to their committed participation in a continuing education program and their real-life application of what they're learning.

Going Toward Type B Behavior and Your Dreams

You need to understand the characteristics of Type A and Type B personalities as part of your plan to reduce your stress. You need to understand the benefits of being a Type B and adopt those traits as much as you can.

In case you're at all concerned about the quality of your life now and in the future, your best bet is to be seriously committed to creating the life you've dreamed of. In the process of learning Type B behavior and growing into it day by day, it's likely you'll be transitioning from qualities that may be offensive and pressure inducing, to more of a calming, confidence-inducing, sincerely caring approach.

To get what you want may require a change in your career, lifestyle, or something else. You'll be gaining more control over your life, thus reducing your stress. You'll need to continue or acquire the habits of regular exercise, eating right, and taking vitamins, minerals, and food supplements—which are also key ingredients to living a healthier, more successful life. We'll cover more on this later. As always, consult with your family physician to determine what he or she recommends in this regard.

As someone once said, "Be prepared to cross the bridge to the life you've always dreamed of. Let go of the stress of not living the life you want. Be in harmony with your innermost desires and become the person you were created to be."

Chapter Three

Exercise Your Way To A Sound Mind and Body

"Be healthy so you can be more productive and successful and enjoy each day of your life more."

How Can a Positive Attitude and Regular Exercise Help You?

Your mind affects your body, and your body affects your mind. They act as a whole and are equally important. For example, a sound body is needed for an alert mind. A positive attitude helps you realize the importance of both, and regular exercise, as approved by your physician, can help you to have a sound body. Any suggestions given here are not to be considered medical guidance. They're just activities that have worked for me and many others. Always check with your family doctor for specific medical guidance.

It is a well-known fact that a positive attitude leads to positive thoughts and great self-csteem. These elements, together with a proper diet and regular exercise, can help you to improve the state of your body and your mind, and their functions, thus improving the quality of your life.

Many people wonder why they don't feel so great much of the time. Many people have developed failure-inducing habits that make it difficult for them to get and stay fit. They don't exercise regularly—except in moving food from their plate to their mouths, that is! They eat rich, sugary, fat-producing foods, and often eat too much too fast with little, if any, attention to a balanced diet. They have a catch as catch can attitude. They just stuff some food in their face on the run.

Exercise alone will not work miracles. To get best results, you need to combine regular exercise with a heart-healthy diet—one that is low in saturated fats, cholesterol, and sodium. With such a diet, a regular, physician-monitored exercise program will benefit your heart in most cases (unless your heart is permanently damaged). Keep in mind that heart disease is the number one killer, at least in the U. S. So for maximum health and success, you need to pay careful attention to what you're doing to keep this vital organ in good working order. The quality of your life, especially as you get older, largely depends on it.

Dieting, without exercise, causes the loss of muscle and water weight as well as some fat loss. However, consistent exercise will help burn fat and keep you from regaining the weight you have lost by adopting healthy eating habits. Notice I said habits. That's the missing piece for many yo-yo dieters. They never got into the habit of consistently exercising and eating a balanced diet of nutritious food in the right quantities to maintain their new slim self. Healthy eating, along with sticking to a physician-recommended exercise program, is the most effective way for most people to control their weight while helping their heart.

I have written regular or consistent in most of my references to exercise. This means at least 30 to 40 minutes, four days a week, 52 weeks a year, for the balance of your life. Of course, again, check with your physician first on this. They can make specific recommendations in line with your particular needs.

But I Don't Have Time...

You may ask, "When am I going to find the time for regular exercise?" Never! You won't *find* the time. You need to *take* the time, i.e., *invest* it! Isn't it true that, as challenging as it may be, you somehow find time to do the things you really want to do? In the past you may have taken time for a two-hour lunch, spent time watching the negative talk shows and situation comedies on TV, or doing many other nonproductive tasks that don't contribute to your financial future. Why not start taking time now for something that can help you succeed?

Making exercise a priority is the first step. Committing to a program and investing time in it is the next step. I used the word investing because exercise is an investment in yourself and your success as a contributing human being. Keep in mind the words of Dr. Edward Stanley: "Those who think they have no time for bodily exercise will sooner or later have to find time for illness."

Get yourself some good walking shoes or sneakers. Set your alarm clock an hour or so earlier in the morning. Early morning is a beautiful and refreshing time for exercise and taking a brisk walk. Put a continuing education tape in a portable audio cassette player and put on the earphones. You can be educating and motivating yourself at the same time as you're becoming healthier and invigorated!

There may be times when you believe you're too tired to exercise. However, some exercise is probably just what you need to help relieve your mental fatigue and stress. Once you start a program you'll have a good feeling in your body. It'll also give you a more alert mind that will help you be more productive and better able to cope with any challenges that arise.

Establish the exercise habit, a beneficial positive habit that will be a part of your routine for the rest of your life. Make a commitment to follow your program and the benefits will be obvious. You'll experience a tremendous feeling of self-mastery, joy and freedom as you exercise. It's a great feeling to exert self-control and do the right thing. What could be more productive than building a sound body to enhance your well being, while strengthening your heart? Remember that you could have all the success in the world but without your good health, you won't enjoy it nearly as much, or perhaps at all—depending on your condition.

A more few positive benefits of regular exercise are:

♦ It helps to lower high blood pressure.

- It increases HDL (good cholesterol) in your blood.
- Your resting heart rate will decrease, enabling your heart to work less than it otherwise would.
- It burns fat to lose weight and helps you maintain a healthy weight.
- Your appetite is decreased because of your higher metabolism.
- It improves your body shape by reducing body fat.
- It helps to relieve anger, depression, and anxiety.
- You'll be in better spirits and be better able to take control of your life.
- It reduces your stress level—a major factor in causing illness in your body.

Physically Fit People Handle Stress Better

There are people who have a natural ability to handle stress. Just as there are differences in other traits—such as hair and skin colors, height and weight, build and intelligence—there's also a difference in everyone's ability to tolerate and manage stress. A person who is physically fit is stronger, and therefore, can withstand stress far better than those who aren't.

Dr. Malcolm Carruthers writes that "The combination of a high level of emotional activity, together with a low level of physical activity deranges body chemistry and is the major cause of heart disease." How many people do you know who fit that profile? Do you?

What Is an Effective Exercise Program?

There are some misconceptions concerning what makes an effective exercise program. The key ingredient is to have continuous activity that increases your heart rate to a safe level for 20 to 40 minutes. Exercises that don't maintain the increase in your heart rate—those that give you short periods of high activity followed by periods of low activity, such as weightlifting, golf, tennis, baseball, football, and bowling—aren't good substitutes for the continuous aerobic types of exercise.

Aerobic exercise can be brisk walking, running, jogging, rowing, cycling, and swimming. I find that a 40-minute brisk walk at a pace of a 13 minute mile or 135 paces per minute, increases my heart rate to my target level. Your target level is the maximum you need to achieve and sustain during exercise, and it depends on your resting rate. Be sure to establish this with your doctor's supervision.

When the weather is cold, windy, hot, or humid, I ride a stationary bike or walk a treadmill for the same period at the same pace. You could listen to a continuing education tape or read a personal development book at the same time!

However, you may prefer, as some people do, to walk outside —regardless of the weather! (You can still take your portable audio tape player and listen to a continuing ed tape.)

Warning: don't start an exercise program until you have your doctor's approval.

Exercise can improve the function of your heart and the efficiency of your cardiovascular system. Even so, a minimum of a five-minute warm-up period prior to exercise and a ten-minute cool down afterward are essential.

A warm-up allows your heart and cardiovascular system time to adjust. It also helps supply the blood and oxygen required by your body during exercise. If you have a damaged heart, surrounding blood vessels and arteries, it's even more important to do this warm-up to accommodate the extra demands of exercise.

Light calisthenics and stretching loosens your muscles, and helps prevent the damage that could result if you would pick up your pace too quickly. Start slowly and gradually increase your pace. The slow progression helps to protect your heart and circulatory system as it works harder to meet the increasing demands you're placing on it.

Cooling down allows your body to slow down gradually following the exercise. Stretching reduces muscle tightness induced by exertion and gives your cardiovascular system a chance to readjust. Let any perspiration evaporate rather than toweling it off, since it provides natural cooling. Delay taking a hot shower or eating solid foods for at least 30 minutes. Drink plenty of fluids to replenish those lost.

My Good Physical Condition Probably Saved My Life

I started exercising 35 years ago, but I didn't use it to gear my program toward helping my heart to be healthy like I do today. I started back then because I wanted to lose weight, like a lot of people do. Then later, I read that exercise is good for both your body and your mind.

When I had my heart attack a few years ago, my doctors told me the fact that I was in good physical condition was a major reason why I survived it. My illness was caused by the blockage of the left descending coronary artery that had apparently been gradually closing for some time. However, amazingly, an EKG (electrocardiogram) taken six months before my attack was totally normal!

The point is, if I hadn't exercised for all those years, even though my exercise was limited in scope, I may have died as a result of that attack. I now do cardiovascular exercises as I described earlier. This program was recommended by my cardiologist, and it consisted of three one-hour sessions each week at a cardiac rehabilitation center where I slowly worked into the program I now use on my own. Your physician can recommend an exercise program to suit your needs. It can be simple to do, yet crucial to your overall well-being and perhaps, like me, your survival. It's definitely worth it!

Many hospitals have a cardiac rehab program for patients with a history of heart disease, diabetes, high blood pressure, and high cholesterol levels. After completing six months of such a monitored program, I still continue to follow their recommendations for maximum effectiveness. I check my pulse rate before, during, and after exercise to be sure I don't exceed my target rate. Your physician can teach you how to check your pulse rate.

Most people can improve their chances for a happy, positive, and healthy life by simply making a few important changes in their habits. In most cases, two of the most consequential changes you can make are in your diet and exercise habits. Schedule time for a systematic program. Thirty minutes a day could, along with improved eating habits, make quite a positive difference in your health and in your life overall. Your increased and more effective productivity could more than make up for the time and energy you invest in making these changes.

Many business owners and other leaders now realize the importance of physical fitness to productivity and have established programs for their executives and other employees. If that's the case where you work, join in on the fun and help your body and mind stay fit and strong. It could pay big dividends! You could probably even fit it in over your lunch period. If not, as we talked about before, maybe you could simply take a brisk walk at lunch. You'll soon be developing a new, fun, and rewarding *habit*—a new pattern of behavior that you'll be doing almost automatically, without conscious thought. Then it becomes easier to *do* than not to do!

Here's something for you to consider...

"I am your constant companion.
I am your greatest helper or your heaviest burden.
I will push you onward or drag you down to failure.
I am completely at your command.

Half the things you do,
You might just as well turn them over to me.
And I will be able to do them quickly and correctly.
I am easily managed; you must merely be
firm with me.

Show me exactly how you want something done,
And after a few lessons, I will do it automatically.
I am the servant of all great people, and, alas, of all
failures as well.

Those who are great, I have made great.
Those who are failures, I have made failures.
I am not a machine, though I work with the precision of a
machine,
Plus the intelligence of a human.

You may run me for profit, or run me for ruin.
It makes no difference to me.

Take me, train me, be firm with me,
And I will put the world at your feet.
Be easy with me and I will destroy you.
Who am I? I am HABIT. "
Author Unknown

As you continue the exercise habit, your overall outlook will be upbeat and positive, and you'll be in a better position to be a self-motivated and successful person. Being in excellent health gives you the energy and vitality you need to do whatever it takes to realize your dreams!

Chapter Four

Motivate Yourself To Greatness

*"Flaming enthusiasm, backed up by horse sense and persistence, is
the quality that most frequently makes for success. "*
Dale Carnegie

What Motivates You?

Motivation is defined as—to provide with a motive. And a
motive is defined as—something (as a need or desire) that causes
a person to act; moving to action.

Contrary to popular belief, most people are not motivated by
money alone. Intangibles such as peace of mind, recognition,
happiness, approval, love, control over your life, and satisfaction
are the greatest motivators of all. No one else can motivate you
long-term. It's something you need to do yourself.

People who win develop the habit of self-motivation. They
learn to talk to themselves in a positive way to motivate
themselves into action, i.e., to *activate* them to do something
beyond the norm.

Dr. Shad Helmstetter, in his book, *What To Say When You
Talk To Yourself,* says, "Unless the programming we received is
erased or replaced with different programming, it will stay with
us permanently and affect and direct everything we do for the rest

of our lives." He teaches us how to talk to ourselves to be successful.

You'll also learn many helpful success-inducing ideas as you read this book, so you can talk to yourself more positively. The winning people also use tools to motivate themselves. They take advantage of the books, tapes, seminars, and other opportunities for growth that their leaders recommend. They are hungry for their dreams to come true. How about you? Are you hungry?

Several positive ingredients are key factors in helping you gain and maintain your personal motivation to take action. The most essential of these are desire, faith, belief, love of people, enthusiasm, and persistence.

Although desire is at the top of the list, you also need the other elements to take your desire and follow it up with consistent appropriate action to have a productive, fulfilling, and happy life.

Desire is more than wishing or hoping for something to happen. Someone who just wishes and hopes for results, rather than taking concrete action, is undoubtedly a person who watches things happen. Most people, unfortunately, fall into this category.

The person who makes things happen, has a strong, unrelenting, burning desire coupled with belief and persistence. They have faith, enthusiasm, and love for people as they persistently blast through the obstacles and take ownership of the title of this book—*if it is to be, it's up to me*. It's *your* dream and *your* responsibility to make it *your* reality.

How Much Do You Want Your Dream?

Without desire, not much, if anything, happens. Once you have established a desire for your dream in your mind and heart, of course you need to follow through with a definite plan of action to reach your goal. Desire alone won't make it miraculously appear! That's just wishful thinking. The action and perhaps sacrifice that accomplishing your goal requires is the price you need to pay.

Are you willing to pay the price? If so, perhaps your mentor or leader can help you develop an action plan. Successful people are dreamers—people of vision. They mentally picture what they really want to accomplish—their dream. This helps them generate a burning desire that serves as the trigger that fires them up and sets them into motion toward fruition of their dream.

What's Your Belief Level?

You need belief to stir up your passion to make your dream an obsession. Open your mind to accept it. Become super-charged with belief and impassioned with your dream. Be willing to step outside the box your thinking has kept you in. A closed mind with preconceived thoughts will not nurture a strong belief.

Continue to open your mind to embrace and fine-tune your thinking to the vast number of possibilities that stretch before you. As you grow, your belief will become stronger and stronger, igniting the passion within you to make real the dream that's so near and dear to your heart.

You also need to believe in and respect yourself, because confidence and self-esteem are key components for belief and desire to work as partners.

As you build your business or profession, and participate in a continuing education program, you can grow your self-esteem and confidence. This will help fire up your belief. As you do so, you can associate with and support others in doing so as well.

You'll continue to attract more success-oriented, positive-thinking people as you lead the way by your powerful positive example. It's a fun, challenging process. True leaders, and those aspiring to be so, are always upgrading their skills to serve more effectively. How about you? What are you doing to be a leader in your field?

When you have a strong belief and a burning desire for achievement, you can accomplish your goals. Any fear of failure and feeling that your goals are impossible to achieve will be history when you truly have a powerful belief and desire. You're then focusing on what *can be done,* rather than what you may have thought in the past *couldn't be done.* This is a positive achievement-inducing mentality that can pay you big dividends. As George Reeves is known for saying, "Knock the 't' off the can't."

Make Persistence Your Middle Name!

Persistence is another key factor in staying motivated. When it's blended with belief, desire, and action, your dream can become reality. Without persistence not much is accomplished. Go forward with resolution doing what you know is right for you in spite of any opposition or warning from others who aren't where you want to be and may just be envious of you.

Don't let anything get in the way of you accomplishing your goals. Do everything necessary to resolve any situation that threatens to thwart your diligent efforts. Stay focused on your previously decided-upon direction. A certain doggedness and perseverance to stay the course and to do whatever it takes describes the persistent person. They reset their goals, if necessary, until they get it done.

How Action-Oriented Are You?

Are you the kind of person who regularly talks about doing great things yet fails to follow through? Do you walk your talk? Are you a pacesetter? Did you take charge, "put your foot down," and start taking action on your dream?

No matter what your habits have been in the past, and we all have some unskillful behaviors to work on, you can become a mover and a shaker—starting now. It's as simple as taking one tiny step in the direction of your dream. It could be just writing it down.

If you haven't written your dream on a piece of paper, perhaps in your day-planner, I dare you to go ahead and do it now. Begin with "my dream is…."

Your burning desire, coupled with your belief, persistence, and appropriate consistent action will, when strongly and positively directed, result in the personal motivation you need to carry you onward to the realization of your dreams.

THE DIMENSIONS OF GREATNESS

No one can know the potential,
of a life that is committed to win;

With courage, the challenge it faces
To achieve great success in the end!

So explore the Dimensions of Greatness,
And BELIEVE that the world CAN be won;
By a mind that is fully committed,
KNOWING the task can be done!

Your world has no place for the skeptic,
No room for the DOUBTER to stand;
To weaken your firm resolution,
That you CAN EXCEL in this land!

We must have VISION TO SEE our potential,
And FAITH TO BELIEVE what we see;
Then COURAGE TO ACT with conviction,
To become what God MEANT us to be!

So possess the strength and the courage,
To conquer WHATEVER you choose;
It's the person WHO NEVER GETS STARTED,
That is destined FOREVER to lose!
                                    Heartsill Wilson

Are You Positive and Excited?

Many years ago, I attended my first seminar on personal motivation. It was valuable because it reinforced the success principles I had been following in my career. They encouraged positive thinking and going in the direction of your dreams. They spurred us on with an encouraging "I did it and you can do it too," message. Their goal was to help us have a happier, more exciting, fulfilling, prosperous, significant, and overall better life.

They used an exciting tone of voice and words such as wonderful, terrific, fired up, outstanding, great, fantastic, super, and excellent. Using such power-packed positive words and an upbeat tone of voice as a part of your everyday language can have an enormous impact on the quality of your life.

How do most people respond to, "How are you today"? They generally give you a low-energy blah tone response of "Not bad,"

"Comme ci, comme ca (so, so)," or "Okay." Whenever the weather isn't sunny and clear, you're likely to hear "Isn't it a lousy day?" In the summer here in the U.S., many people complain that it's too hot, while in the winter they say it's too cold. When it's raining they say it's dreary.

Those phrases focus on the negative rather than the positive aspects of the weather. For example, if it's raining you could say, "We really need this rain," if that's true. Or you could call it liquid sunshine. Or you could decide *not* to comment on the weather and instead focus your attention on the *person* you're talking to. You could sincerely ask them how they are and truly listen to them.

Choose to make a positive difference. If you say and do what the average-thinking person says and does, you'll get average results. Average results aren't what you want—or you wouldn't be reading this book, would you?

So in response to the question "How are you today?" say "Wonderful!" "Sensational!" or "Great!" You'll upgrade and enrich your life by being positive and you may be surprised by the pleasant reactions you're likely to get from others, who respond in kind. I vividly recall such an experience while on a business trip when I was having breakfast at the restaurant of a major motel chain. The hostess greeted me, "How are you this morning?" My enthusiastic response of "Wonderful!" brought a happy smile as she said, "Gee, can it really be that good so early in the morning?"

By using an uplifting tone of voice and positive words and phrases in your responses, in most cases, you will experience cheerful reactions. Brighten other people's day with your optimistic, sunny disposition. Be a people magnet. You may be nurturing a relationship with someone you'll be associating with in some important way in the future. But regardless of whether you'll ever talk to someone again, nonetheless, be an encourager every day.

Consider this. If you agree with the statement "Isn't it a lousy day?" you're not helping the person who thinks this way. Their attitude will only create negativity. They'll get what they expect —the worst. You'd also be reinforcing their negative thoughts in your own mind, which will hurt rather than help you. Therefore, speak only positive words. You may feel uncomfortable and awkward the first few times. But after 21 days of concentration, speaking with a positive focus will become a habit—a wonderful, happy, success inducing habit. You'll be a pleasure to be around and you'll attract other positive thinking people to you, which will be great for building your business or career!

Remember as George Bernard Shaw once said, "The people who get on in this world are the people who get up and look for the circumstances they want and if they can't find them, make them."

You Control Your Thoughts—No Matter What!

There are many books on positive thinking. However, a vast number of people are still doubters as they continue to have negative thoughts. They believe their situation is caused by factors beyond their control. They refuse to take personal responsibility for the part they played in causing the situation they're in. They blame others and do no more than complain about it. So their thinking keeps them stuck.

But the truth is, thinking positive is a choice—no matter what your circumstances may be!

Our environment, some say, is often negative; therefore, they contend it is difficult to have a positive attitude. That's only an excuse. Don't buy it! There are far too many examples of people of all backgrounds, income levels, race, religion, and physical and mental challenges, who have used a positive mental attitude to their advantage.

There are leaders throughout the world, especially those who started with nothing and rose up the ranks, who are among those people. They developed a mental toughness and fought like crazy to rise above any negative effects their environment or any other challenges may have presented. They are successful and lead rewarding, fulfilling lives. Such people are an inspiration to many who previously thought they were locked into a depressing negative environment. They may look like they're lucky, once they've overcome their obstacles. But as Emily Dickinson once said, "Luck in not chance. It's toil. Fortune's expensive smile is earned."

My guess is that you want to be happy, as most people do. Am I right? If so, keep in mind what Dale Carnegie once said, "Remember, happiness doesn't depend upon who you are or what you have; it depends solely upon what you think."

Here's something else to think about. All progress would stop if the world was run by those who said it couldn't be done!

Most people thought electricity was impossible. Knowing what you know now, that may be hard to believe. However, the same thing was thought about the telephone, the railroads, flying, putting men on the moon, and hundreds of other inventions and accomplishments. What if the people behind these developments had a negative can't do attitude? What if they had taken the advice of the people putting them and their project down? Where would we all be?

You not only need to monitor and control your thoughts about your goals and dreams, but you need to get and stay positive about yourself and your abilities. Belief in yourself and a can do attitude are two of the most important attributes you can have - as you work toward your dreams and goals, which may seem unrealistic to many now. People who put you down may call you crazy when you start something new. Then after you succeed, they simply say you're lucky! This just seems to be the way of the average people of the world.

Do you want to rise to leadership (or higher leadership) in your organization? Do you want to make a positive difference in the lives of others? Have you noticed that people who rise to the top are, by and large, kind, considerate people? They generally have a great attitude, care about people, and do their best to help others succeed. They tend to follow the idea that you can have everything in life you want after you have helped enough other people get what they want.

Successful people expect success and through enough consistent appropriate action, they achieve it. Sure they fail along the way—but they keep going. They expect the best of themselves and encourage others to do their best too. They don't make excuses—taking full responsibility for their life and the results they achieve. They refuse to play the "blame game." They know it leads nowhere, and they encourage others to take responsibility too.

True achievers realize that, as someone once shared, "Success is the *progressive realization* of a worthwhile dream or goal." It's not just an end point. They enjoy the present as much as possible, since it's a part of the trip along the way! They develop to the point where they are confident and sure of themselves and where they're going. (A few have confidence in the beginning. But many need to develop it as they go along.) They have a deep abiding love for people and the welfare of others. They realize it's important to give back to society some part of what they receive.

A positive attitude attracts success whereas *a negative attitude deflects it.* It doesn't matter if the person is young or old, short or tall, fat or thin. And race and religion have nothing to do with their chances of success either. Successful people simply and absolutely expect to succeed, are committed to it, and do whatever it takes to make it happen. They don't give up their quest. They, as Winston Churchill so aptly put it, "Never, never, never give in...."

American playwright and director Moss Hart once said, "Can success change the human mechanism so completely between one dawn and another? Can it make one feel taller, more alive, handsomer (or prettier), uncommonly gifted, and indomitably secure with the certainty that this is the way life will always be? Yes it can and it does!"

Plan Your Work and Work Your Plan

Now that's certainly a well worn phrase that most everyone could agree with—in principle, anyway. However, only 5 to 10 percent of all people actually practice it, while many others may plan but never take the necessary follow-up action. Most people do neither!

Here's an example to illustrate...

Bob was an insurance agent in the agency I operated. He always appeared to be highly motivated after every Friday morning sales meeting. He invariably made what seemed to be outstanding plans for the future, and left the office with what appeared to be confidence, enthusiasm, and an effective plan. However, Bob's plan never worked. Why? Because he didn't get out of bed on Monday morning to start working it. He failed simply because he didn't carry out his plan. He hadn't learned how to motivate himself to take action.

Self-motivated people not only plan their work. They follow through with positive action. Their motivation leads to *activation*, which is a key ingredient to success in any endeavor. We all need to do the walking, not just the talking.

I once thought that, as a leader, I was a good motivator. For years I kept getting reasonable results from people with average or below average productivity levels. But while they occasionally achieved outstanding results, what they accomplished overall wasn't acceptable. They were inconsistent in their personal motivation and this led to peaks and valleys in their productivity. I just can't imagine they were happy with their achievement level— I *know* I wasn't!

Surround Yourself with Motivated People

I finally came to realize that I needed to surround myself with self-motivated people if I wanted to accomplish my goals. I came to the conclusion that my attempts to motivate others were frequently short-lived. In many cases, these people simply had little or no self-motivation. Short-duration motivation can be achieved by an inspiring message, sharing stimulating information, and by instilling a sense of faith and hope that they can do it too.

Striking fear in people's hearts is *not* the way to motivate them. It will eventually alienate them.

Sustained motivation, though, comes from within the person. This is a key point to remember, and is the missing link for most people. They may get fired up at a weekend seminar, but unless they have a strong internal desire, they fail to follow through on Monday. That's when the true test of their commitment greets them.

My philosophy changed as I surrounded myself with people I didn't need to motivate. I modified my recruiting and selection procedures so to assure that the people I hired already had a history of personal motivation. I could then direct my energy to create a positive environment in which they could excel. I was then also able to invest more time developing marketing strategies to move the agency onward and upward.

If you are someone who is not currently self-motivated, the great news is you can change, as long as you have the desire to do so. With perseverance, sacrifice, and commitment, along with a positive attitude, we can all stay motivated when left to our own devices. Perhaps it's time to prove we finally mean business. Anyone can change their habits and attitudes. And as previously mentioned, it takes only 21 days to accomplish. Always look at yourself and others as you and they can be, not as you and they currently are.

Always set a level of positive expectation for both yourself and others to rise to. And remember your excellent example is your greatest teacher!

How to Become Self-Motivated

Here are some ideas that can assist anyone to become self-motivated. These principles are not only useful for your entrepreneurial or career success, but for all relationships in your life:

- Build relationships on mutual trust and respect, and create win-win situations so everyone benefits.
- Recognize the potential of others and the untapped talent they have. If they are willing to develop their skills and abilities, help them do it.
- Establish a plan for greatness by writing down your dreams. Include everything you want out of life. Then attach a date to each dream—making each a goal—and write them down. You may want to do this with your mentor or leader.
- Become committed by planning your course of action and strengthening your willingness to pay the price.

♦ Listen and watch others you're communicating with in their verbal and nonverbal communication. Discover what you can learn about them through you observation and ask them questions about what they're saying. Always be honest and sincere with others. *People don't care how much you know until they know how much you care.*

♦ Use positive reinforcement to help others build on their strengths. Compliment people sincerely. Tolerate mistakes with empathy and help others grow through their weaknesses. Be kind, compassionate, honest, and encouraging.

♦ Cope with temporary setbacks by constantly focusing on your goals and dreams and what you're doing to pursue them. Know that a delay isn't a denial.

Self-confidence and self-esteem are fundamental qualities of a self-motivated person. Always be the kind of person whom you would want as a friend or business associate. Always conduct yourself in your business or career and personal activities as though you are someone you'd like to do business or associate with personally.

You Only Have One Chance to Make a Good First Impression

Effective communication is another important component of personal motivation. You relate to others in both verbal and nonverbal ways. In many cases, your nonverbal communication gives others their first and possibly their most lasting impression. It includes how you present yourself to others, i.e., your mannerisms, grooming, posture, and how you greet someone, e.g., the words you use, your attitude, the firmness of your handshake, your facial expression, tone of voice, and eye contact. All of these things need to reflect a positive forward thinking you. It's essential in order for others to have confidence in and want to associate with you.

When you shake hands, make sure your grip is firm but not vise-like, and look the person directly in the eye. A weak, limp handshake is viewed by most as a sign of a person with wimpy (weak, timid) characteristics—someone without confidence or self-esteem. You show a lack of interest in the other person if you look elsewhere while shaking their hand or later as you're talking with them. Focus on *them* and ignore potential distractions.

When you look good, you generally feel good about yourself. What you're wearing can be a significant statement of nonverbal communication. It certainly does not change your philosophies or ideals, but it can send a positive or negative signal. For example, say you dress casually (blue jeans/tee shirt) as a business owner who has a home-based business. However, you've scheduled an appointment to meet with a prospect at a local major hotel restaurant.

You know the person you're meeting is a corporate leader and will be traveling from his office, most likely in an expensive three-piece suit. So, even though you may not want to, you would be safest to dress in business attire too. It may be true that you have the self-esteem to dress casually—that's great, but casual attire can create casualness that may not be conducive to a particular situation. You may not be taken seriously and therefore be unable to communicate as effectively as you'd like.

Would your confidence in a doctor or attorney you're meeting for the first time be diminished if they conducted their business in a sport shirt, slacks, shorts, or sandals? Due to all of your different viewpoints, some of you probably said yes and others said no! But just think about it.

A cocktail or two at lunch may be popular in some business circles, but it can destroy your chances of success in most. Most people will lose confidence and question your credibility at the smell of alcohol on your breath. It doesn't matter how much or how little you've had to drink. This nonverbal signal can be disastrous in building relationships. Stay away from alcohol. It often sends a negative signal and you'll also start losing your mental sharpness —which you're likely to need at your meeting. Otherwise you may agree to things and even sign papers you wouldn't have signed if you had not been drinking. Why not have a nice safe cup of coffee or soda?

Other positive nonverbal signs are clean fingernails, clean and well-groomed hair, clean, fresh, light scent (i.e., no body odor—amazingly, some people don't take a daily both or shower or use deodorant antiperspirant), no facial hair, and a shine on your shoes. Of course, never smoke in anyone's presence without requesting permission. Better yet, don't smoke at all! Besides being harmful to your health, it could be an immediate turnoff to those you're with.

Since enthusiasm and a positive attitude are contagious, always exhibit them in both your nonverbal and verbal communications. Both are important parts of having a successful discussion with or a presentation to anyone.

You may appear authoritative pulling rank and alienate some people if you sit behind your desk. However, if you want to eliminate this risk and you really want to communicate, come from behind your desk, pull up a chair, and participate on a more equal person to person basis with them. This generally makes for a more relaxed, comfortable presentation or discussion, as you'll be physically closer to the other person, eliminating the barrier a desk creates to communication. It's likely your visitor will be more at ease and therefore more willing to open their mind to your thoughts, suggestions, or opportunity.

Six Tips for Improving Your Self-Confidence, Self-Esteem, and Personal Motivation

1. Act enthusiastic. Smile! Walk with purpose even if you're only going for a cup of coffee. Be conscious of your posture when sitting and walking.

2. Work to improve your skills and abilities regularly and consistently. Maintain the thought that you will be a better leader (or whatever you're striving to be), next month or next week, than you are today. Concentrate on improving your voice, listening skills, posture, memory, routine, and all else that needs fine-tuning that affects your life and relating with others.

3. Get things done—particularly the important things you've been putting off for a while that will help you achieve your

dreams and goals. For example, call everyone on your prospect or customer list! A sense of accomplishment helps to improve your outlook. Get to work or start your daily chores earlier than normal for a week or so to catch up on lingering projects.
4. Always speak in positive terms and suggest that your associates do the same. An enthusiastic solution and possibility-oriented attitude and behavior will accomplish a great deal more than a pessimistic, problem focused, apathetic attitude and behavior
5. Learn more about what you do, whether it's product knowledge, leadership skills, inter-personal relationships, or something else. Knowledge can help you improve your performance and self-confidence. Keep practicing what you have to do. Always be learning and growing!
6. Set goals and focus on your dream. Make your goals challenging yet do-able, so you need to stretch to reach them. Reset them as often as necessary to achieve them. Your attitude will improve when you have something specific to strive for.

Effective personal motivation causes activation and therefore, results to occur. They can be positive or negative, depending on the direction of the motivation. Positive motivation leads to positive action. All you can do is the best you can do. You may get the results you want and you may not. If you don't, reflect on your motivation and actions taken and determine whether you can change the results or not. If not, move on, and let it go. If so, learn from it, begin again, only more smartly, if possible!

Truly Successful People Are Self-Motivated, Humble, Have Wisdom, and Are Self-Disciplined
Some of the significant characteristics of positive self-motivated people are humility, wisdom, and self-discipline.
Humility is recognizing that you don't accomplish anything alone. People who are ego-driven and tend to brag about themselves need to remember what I shared earlier—people don't care how much you know until they know how much you care. You being a caring person toward others is key to building strong lasting relationships, business and personally.

Realize that you will make mistakes in life—no one's behavior is perfect. Mistakes are just events—they are not who you are! Self-respect and humility will, however, bring you back to reality and back on a positive track after you have made mistakes or failed in some way. With these traits, you can stay on the positive track and achieve the measure of success and happiness you deserve.

An important aside: achievements that result from illegal or immoral means have no place in your life. Remember that—especially if you're tempted to short cut the success process. Never sacrifice your values just to meet a goal! It's not worth it.

Humility is essential, especially when you accomplish major goals that put you in the limelight. As others are congratulating you, it takes true humility to acknowledge the role others played in your victory. It's tempting just to bask in the glow of adoration.

It's important to share the glory—give credit where credit is due. How much did you really put into this effort? Does some or even much of the credit belong to others: your spouse, children, friends, employees, business associates, mentor, or leaders? If so, acknowledge these people publicly, if possible. Build the people up who supported and helped you, and they'll be likely to want to help you achieve even more!

Wisdom is a true understanding of people and life. It is being a clear thinker with an excellent sense of things and the ability to make sound decisions. It's also having good common sense, which seems to be uncommon! It's simply perception and reasoning while using good judgment.

Self-motivated people who are successful long-term have developed the wisdom to make sound decisions by using common sense. This wisdom comes both by their own trial and error and what they learn from others. They also have an understanding of and appreciation for the positive factors that influence their lives.   They take little or nothing for granted.

Self-discipline is following through with what you have promised yourself in a specific area: time and activity management; living your values; delivering goods or services on time; sticking to your heart-healthy diet; or adhering to the exercise program you know will improve your attitude, reduce stress, and give you a fit body and a more peaceful mind.

Being self-disciplined isn't having the rigid, strict lifestyle you might be imagining. It actually allows you to have more time for relaxation and family than you otherwise might have experienced. You deliberately block out time to do the things you specifically need to do to achieve your goals. And not only that, you're actually *doing* these key tasks. You can feel free to schedule in some for-fun-only activities. You're not wishy-washy—consistently procrastinating taking necessary actions—like many people are. Therefore, you can pack more into your life.

Self-discipline is having a plan—an agenda with a definite purpose—and a solid commitment to take positive action to reach your goals.

It's deferring instant gratification to attain a dream or goal. For instance, you may prefer to play golf or tennis, but you promised your spouse you'd build your business or career. So you invest your time wisely to fulfill your promise.

Self-discipline is a prerequisite for personal motivation. You need to practice it, improve it, and live it (walk your talk) to accomplish your goals and dreams, while sticking to your values.

If you have any weakness in any or all of these characteristics—humility, wisdom, and self-discipline—work hard to bring them into focus. You were born with self-motivation, but it could have been lost as you progressed through life.

In the past, have you blamed things like a poor home environment, inadequate education, or an absence of direction for any lack of motivation you may have? If you're experiencing little if any self-motivation, the great news is it can be restored by taking total responsibility for everything in your life. Shift your focus, activate yourself to take corrective action step by step, and think only positive thoughts. Keep taking positive actions until you have achieved the results and the success you really want.

Your self-motivation and activation to greatness will not only enrich your personal life, but also enhance your success in your business or career. It's what leaders and other achievers do around the world. Smooth the road to your goals and dreams by your own unrelenting personal motivation.

Chapter Five

The Relationship Of Your Attitude To Your Career Or Business

"Maturity begins to grow when you can sense your concern for others out-weighing your concern for yourself."
John MacNaughton

Keep on Sharing

Whatever your destination in life, you need to constantly network and share yourself and your ideas with others. If you keep what you know all to yourself, you won't help anyone and you'll never succeed.

You may have been the one who shared the idea with your spouse of spending the rest of your life together in marriage. It's likely that you shared your feelings and whims with your parents or caretakers, almost from your first day of life. You've shared your capabilities and talents with your first and any subsequent employers. You may have shared a business concept with others and they decided to join you as a business associate. Since sharing is such an integral part of life, you need to make the most of your life by sharpening your sharing skills. This, along with a positive attitude, will help enable you to reach higher goals and live your dream.

The KASH Principle

Early in my career, I learned an acronym that played a large part in my development as a top salesman, manager, and leader in my profession. It also helped me throughout my involvement in civic, charitable, church, and business associations, and it can help you in building your business or profession.

Much study, research, and observation over the years went into developing the methods and techniques of truly successful people. One of the constants with these people is they are all good at sharing ideas and building relationships.

The acronym **KASH** can be used to highlight the principles necessary for success:

- ♦ **K** is for knowledge
- ♦ **A** is for attitude
- ♦ **S** is for skills
- ♦ **H** is for habits

Which of these attributes do you believe are essential to success? All are important; however, one is decisive. Which one? Let's examine them.

Knowledge can be acquired by most anyone, given enough time. There are countless "how to" books written to assist you in gaining knowledge of anything you want to learn. Unfortunately, there are some people who make their product, service, or opportunity appear to be complicated. They apparently do this to impress a customer or prospect with their knowledge. As you may have discovered, this approach doesn't work!

Learn To Express, Not Impress

I recall going on a group interview some years ago with a regional group insurance representative. We made our presentation by showing the prospective client how our product would solve his problem: to provide adequate life and health coverage to his employees at a reasonable and affordable cost to his company. Our solution conformed to their needs and we made the proposal easy for the client to understand. He purchased our plan and then confided to us that he had been shopping around for some time. The problem was, he shared, other salespeople had made the solution appear very complicated and confusing. Therefore, since he couldn't understand it, he refused to buy it.

This reminds me of the well-known "KISS" principle. Keep It Simple and Straightforward. You can't go wrong using this approach in dealing with others.

Knowledge is power when it is shared, and it can be put to use in a positive or negative way. It can also be dormant and therefore of absolutely no value. It doesn't do any good unless you share it!

As an analogy, consider a large powerful engine in a racecar. It can be operated at full throttle but is of absolutely no value unless a relatively small but consequential universal joint connects it to and shares it with the drive shaft. When it does, the wheels turn and the machine moves.

You, with your powerful knowledge and enthusiasm, are the universal joint. Share what you've learned in your business career with others, otherwise it is of little value. Your ability to do this is a key factor on your road of success.

Put Your Skills Into Action

Skills can be developed or acquired by training and experience, then sharpened and put into action. You can learn the information you need to know in your career or business perhaps through books, audio and video tapes, seminars, training sessions, the Internet, CD-ROMs, or other methods. You can grow to understand what you've learned so you can share it with others. This could include facts and figures, as well as technical and people skills.

If you do not pay attention and learn to understand people, however, and your only focus is on the cold hard facts without considering the needs and desires of your prospects and customers, nobody will accept what you're sharing. Most people make decisions based on emotion backed-up by logic. They'll only do something if they have a reason—*a dream!*

Skill is the ability to effectively use the knowledge you have. Understanding and judgment are needed to make intelligent use of knowledge. This comes with observation and experience. There are basic human wants and frailties that influence most people's decisions. This makes it important for you to do your best to completely understand them as people, as much as possible. You can then share how your product, service, or opportunity could fulfill their wants and dreams and at the same time, diminish the negative results of their frailties, i.e., help them get out of debt, perhaps. Strive to achieve excellence as you practice your skills.

Remember what Helen Keller once said, "When we do the best we can, we never know what miracle is wrought in our life or in the life of another."

Habits Are Like Being on Autopilot

We are all creatures of *habit* and some are positive while others are negative. Fortunately, as we discussed before, we can change our habits through our deliberate conscious effort over time. Habits require little or no conscious thought once they become "embedded" into your subconscious mind. They are like an autopilot. This is great as long as they're beneficial habits!

Many people possess these three parts of the "KASH" principle: Knowledge, Skills, and Habits. Successful people also have the fourth one...

So, What's the Main Ingredient?

One key ingredient remains, however, that is most decisive and makes the principle work. What is this key ingredient?

It's *Attitude*—a positive mental attitude.

It matters little what your career or business is; having a great attitude will help you succeed and having a poor attitude will almost guarantee failure. For one thing, business is built to a large extent on relationships. If a person has "stinking thinking," how can they be successful?

For example, a truck driver, a waitress, a teacher, an executive, a bank teller, a homemaker, a parent, a policeman, and a salesperson all need to have a positive attitude to have a favorable impact on their future. This may seem so obvious. But amazingly, a lot of people simply don't get it. They keep dumping negativity on others and somehow expect to get positive results!

Consider this: we are all salespersons, in a sense, because we're always sharing ourselves, our ideas, talents, and perhaps our dreams, with others. Many times throughout the day, it's likely we have the opportunity to sell ourselves to others or ruin the "sale." For example, if we care about and listen to others, we're more likely to achieve a win-win outcome in any particular relationship. Our attitude is central in all we do.

Here's a list of six indispensable attitudes that are fundamental regardless of your current primary or secondary occupation:

♦ You need to have a positive attitude toward the industry(ies) you're involved with—your job(s), and/or business(es). Sure you may want to make a change; that's fine. But in the meantime, it's important to do your best to look for the good and to be pleasant for your own sake and also for the well being of those around you!

♦ You also need to have a positive attitude toward the products, services, and perhaps even an opportunity you have available to share. You need to have complete confidence in the value of these things. If you don't believe in what you are sharing, whatever it may be, how can you reasonably expect your customers or prospects to believe that what you have can help them solve a challenge or even reach their goals and dreams? This requires, in many cases, you actually using the products and services, as appropriate, especially if they're everyday items you use anyway.

Self-use is the key to your ability to heartily recommend something to others. If you're selling something like wheelchairs, and you don't personally need one, you can boost your attitude by talking with some people who have or are successfully using your product and have glowing comments about it.

♦ You need to have a positive attitude toward the company or organization with whom you're connected, and your associates and leaders. You need to believe that you're associated with the best company or organization in the business and that your leaders can lead you (or you lead yourself if you're the top person) in the direction you need to go to reach your goals and make your dreams come true. If this isn't the case, what are you doing it for? A survival attitude will only get you minimal results.

♦ You need to have a positive attitude toward yourself, self-confidence, intact self-esteem, and an unconditional loving attitude toward yourself. How can you respect and care about others if you don't respect and care about yourself? You can't give or share with other people what you don't already have!

♦ You need to have a positive attitude that the people who need and may want your product, service, or opportunity (your market) are approachable and that what you have to offer is in demand.

♦ You need to have a positive attitude toward other people and honestly want to help them. You need to have and show a sincere interest in their welfare and communicate this other-centered attitude to them. A positive attitude is contagious; therefore, people you come in contact with can benefit from your attitude and enthusiasm, regardless of their response to what you're sharing.

How Lack of a Positive Attitude Caused Failure

Here's a dramatic example of how one person who had three elements of the KASH principle but lacked the fourth (attitude) had failed. He was a cum laude graduate of a large, respected college where he had majored in insurance. Because of his educational background and academic record of achievement, the insurance manager who hired him was enthusiastic and confident that he was a prime candidate for success in the position of salesperson.

The challenge was his negative attitude toward himself and others. He had no self-confidence, self-esteem, or enthusiasm.

He never achieved the measure of success he could have had with his Knowledge, Skill, and Habits. Why? A positive Attitude, the decisive ingredient, was missing. Perhaps he didn't realize he was holding himself back because of his negative attitude. Regardless of whether this was the case or not, he never developed a positive attitude. What a tragic waste of talent! He could have excelled if he had only changed his attitude!

Just consider this...

Think

If you think you are beaten, you are.
If you think that you dare not, you don't.
If you like to win, but think you can't,
It's almost certain, you won't.

If you think you'll lose, you've lost.
For out in the world you'll find
Success begins with a fellow's will-
It's all in the state of mind.

If you think you are outclassed, you are.
You've got to think high to rise. You've got to
be sure of yourself before
You can ever win the prize.

Life's battles don't always go
To the stronger or faster man;
But sooner or later the man who wins
Is the man who thinks he can.

What Is "Sharemanship"?

Few people like to sell and no one likes to be "sold." But most everyone likes to buy! The idea of selling is usually interpreted to mean that someone is trying to convince them of something they don't want to do, or push something on to them that they neither need nor want. And because of their general negative association with the idea of selling, many people assume a defensive posture and say no. If you try to sell someone on something, based on *your* reasons, they may say yes, but they'll probably change their mind later. People need to say yes or no for *their* reasons, not yours! As the saying goes, "A man convinced against his will is of the same opinion still." How true!

However, when you sincerely share what you have to offer—be it a product, service, opportunity, or something else—with others, they'll probably get the feeling that you're presenting them with a solution to one or more of their challenges. Or it could be something to help them avoid a challenge(s) in the future, i.e., a preventive measure. You need to do this in as nice a way as you can—*as a friend.*

When you share with someone what you have to offer, you are basically presenting an option or options for them to consider. You want your prospect, customer, or client to see how what you're sharing could help them make their life more enjoyable, overcome an obstacle, or maybe realize a goal or a dream.

Discover the other person's real need or desire by asking them questions and listening carefully to their responses. Focus on how you can help them get what *they* want and need. In some instances, you may not be able to provide what they need. But, if you know someone who may know what *can* help them, suggest they investigate the possibilities with that person. That's all part of honestly caring about others.

Remember that people are creatures of emotion, often with their decisions only faintly backed up by logic. No matter how great what you have to share is, nobody will even consider buying or doing it without first having a reason—a *why* to do so. Focus on their *why.* Unless you're dealing with a very detail-oriented person, you can usually cover the facts, figures, and miscellaneous details later.

When your prospect, customer, or client gets excited about the results they can achieve with what you're sharing—watch them move in your direction. They'll be more inclined to take advantage of what you have to offer when they realize it can help them get what they want. That person needs to have a definite desire that they want to fulfil, perhaps a dream or goal, before you can realistically expect them to go forward. And as the expression goes, "They gotta wanna."

I have used sharemanship where I otherwise would have used salesmanship. When you *share* various solutions, ideas, and dreams with others in a comfortable, enthusiastic way, they will be more receptive than if you just try to sell them based strictly on what *you* think they want and need.

Serving someone in your business or career is best based on sharemanship. It's the ability to meet, take an interest in, understand, befriend, and have compassion for others. First it involves discovering their needs, dreams, or challenges, and sharing what you have to offer them to get what they want. It could be a simple solution to a small household challenge, a major plan to help them achieve a new lifestyle, or anything in between.

Sharemanship is an approach you can use every day to find people and build friendships with them. Depending on their needs and wants, you could potentially share your product(s), service(s), or opportunity with them.

There are four distinct steps to sharemanship—the process of attracting people to serve in your business or career—contacting, inviting, sharing what you have to offer, and following up. Here's a brief explanation of each:

Contacting—*Meeting or Making New Friends*
Contacting involves meeting someone new, and taking a sincere interest in them and their needs and wants. In fact, to cultivate the attitude you need to contact effectively, you may want to call it *meeting or making new friends*—anywhere at anytime. If you can say hi you can meet people! After that, all you need to do is "break the ice" with a positive statement like "Great weather we're having today," or "That's a really nice car," or "What a cute baby," or "That's a really sharp suit."

Whatever it is, just relax with it and be natural and sincere. Then you can continue to get to know the person more by asking open-ended questions. These are questions that require more than just a yes or no answer. For example, you might ask a storeowner, "How did you get into this business?" It's likely one thing will lead to another and, if the person feels comfortable with you, they may even share their life story! People just love it when someone listens to them. Listen and get to know them better and you'll find out what they want and need. This shows them you care and it could be the start of a new friendship. And people are more inclined do business with a friend.

Inviting—*Setting Up an Appointment*

Of course there are a number of opportunities you could be sharing, like the chance for someone to join you as a business partner. Or perhaps you are expanding something like a McDonald's franchise. The most popular, though, are independent home-based businesses, especially those that take advantage of e-commerce and the Internet.

Never share your opportunity with a stranger. Only invite people you've developed a relationship with through the contacting process.

The best way to invite a new friend to *get together* with you is probably over the phone. The purpose of your call is to determine whether they're just complaining or daydreaming, or if they have a sincere interest in doing something about their challenge, goal, or dream. If they seem serious, set up time to get together with them.

Say you own your own business and are looking to bring on some new partners or associates. An invitation could go something like this: "Joe, this is (your name) of (your company's name). We met a couple of weeks ago at the restaurant on the Square, and you mentioned to me that you were looking to move on from your job. Is that still true? Look, I can't promise you anything, but we're expanding a phase of our business operations in the area and considering adding a couple of key people. I'm quite busy, but if you're serious, I have an opening in my schedule to get together with you the week of the 14th, on either Monday or Wednesday evening."

This approach can be varied to suit the individual situation and prospect, making it extremely versatile and flexible.

The most important thing you can do is to "take it away from them," because people often want what they don't think they can have. Never plead with or try to convince anyone through manipulation, or any other negative approach, to get together with you. It simply doesn't work for excellent long-term results.

Remember, you have "the cookie"—something of value to offer them. You don't need any one person to be successful yourself. Don't "fall in love" with someone who appears to be a great prospect. They may not be. Keep going until you find those who have a strong *desire* and sincerely want what you have to offer.

Sharing—*Showing an Opportunity*

Some folks call this an interview. The truth is, if you are sharing an opportunity with a new friend, you need to have the attitude that you're getting together to determine if they truly qualify to be an associate of yours. This is called posturizing.

Don't beg anyone to accept what you have to share. In fact, you want them to know you only have enough time left in your schedule to work with just a few select people who are truly serious about moving on. (That's the truth—isn't it?) You are in the driver's seat of your business and you get to pick who you want to associate with you. To be successful in business, you need to surround yourself with positive, ambitious, upward-thinking people—like you!

The most important aspect of sharing an opportunity is the dream. Focus on what your new friend is really looking for. Ask them what their wants are. Then focus on them and what they want, and how associating with you in business can help them get it. No one will do anything unless they have a strong enough reason. And it's unlikely they will join you in business if they believe they have another way to get what they want.

Another aspect of sharing an opportunity (or products and services, for that matter) is to have fun with it. Show a good sense of humor and don't take yourself too seriously. People like to be around others who are having fun. Show your new friend that associating with you in business can be fun, as well as rewarding!

Put People First—*Your Ability to Work With Others Is Key*
In this computer age, more and more options for sharing an opportunity exist than ever before. Some independent business owners may even use a CD-ROM spark interest in what they have to offer. And the Internet offers almost limitless possibilities for the distribution of products or services. And, in some cases, it can also facilitate signing up new customers or associates.

Now even though computerization can certainly make things easier, remember this: the only way to develop a strong business is to build and maintain relationships with other people. Always consider people first, what you can do to serve them, and the quality of your relationships with them. *That's* what makes or breaks your business or career.

Always care sincerely for those who associate with you. The computer is a wonderful servant but it won't build your relationships—only *you* can do that. Anyone who tries to shortcut the relationship-building process, as challenging as it can be, will shortchange his or her success.

We all still need to learn and grow as people, and treat others compassionately, to be truly successful and happy. It's human nature for all of us to want success to be easy. We want everyone to be a joy to deal with. But our biggest growth and greatest success comes as a result of persistently putting others first, whether they're likeable or not. So embrace the computer as a fine tool to leverage with. But keep in mind that the "magic" is in you. Your ability to work with others to create win-win scenarios, in all areas of your life, is key to your success.

Following Up—*Strike While the Iron's Hot!*
Here are some ideas to consider when scheduling and doing a follow up appointment. It makes sense to "strike while the iron is hot." When you have a prospect who is excited about the opportunity you've shared with them, schedule a follow up appointment soon—within the next day or two, if possible—

Being focused on taking care of business helps you to build momentum and excitement, and attracts more positive thinking people to you. You are focused and moving forward. That's the attitude of those who win.

People who win are like a train moving on—it keeps going regardless of who gets on board or doesn't. This is part of posturizing, and realizing *you* are responsible for your own success. You are not attached to any particular person or people following your lead. You only want people who are honestly looking for more success or income—before you invest time with them.

The more you do, fine-tuning your skills as you go, the more successful you can become. Your success depends largely on your effectiveness in prospecting, bringing on more qualified associates, teaching them your business system—and caring about them once they've come on board. Your success depends on your ability to make friends and share your opportunity with those who have a desire to accomplish more.

Sharing Products or Services

Your approach needs to be different when you're sharing products or services. For one thing, as mentioned earlier, you wouldn't posturize. Instead, you would inquire about and cater to their needs and wants—given, of course, that you can help them with what you're offering. Sharemanship means you "put yourself in their shoes" and empathize with them.

For example, if you are sharing concentrated cleaning products, you might say, "Mary, I understand you have been buying (XX brand name) products for years at the grocery store. What we have here are the same type of products you use everyday. However, they are concentrated. This means that you're no longer paying for water or filler. You're getting the pure product, which not only lasts longer, but saves you money."

Next, you would share a brochure that compares your products to the store brands. Then you could say…

"Mary, you'll also save time with these products. First, they've been tested thoroughly and are so effective they reduce the time you spend cleaning. If you have a cleaning person, the labor savings can reduce the time and therefore the cost of hiring them. They could also do more for you in the same period of time."

And then you could add...

"You can also save time at the grocery store because these products are available either by calling a toll-free telephone number or using the Internet. You even have the option of becoming a preferred customer, if you like. This would enable you to save even more money because you could buy these products at a discounted rate."

Successful Leaders Lead People and Manage Things

A professional, effective, and successful leader leads rather than manages. They lead people and manage things. The greatest responsibility of leaders is to those they lead.

As responsible leaders and parents, we all need to have the values and character traits that will improve our quality of life. Here are several leadership traits that are appropriate for leaders in all areas of life:

◆ Above all, you need a positive attitude because positive thoughts, leading to positive actions, are more likely to bring positive results. It's a chain reaction.

◆ Love needs to be part of your make-up. Be interested in the welfare of all people. Also care about the environment and all creatures.

◆ You need to have sincere enthusiasm to open your mind so that learning can take place. It is contagious, and it can make prospecting, sales, and all other communication and relationship building smoother, more effective, and more fun.

◆ You need to show creativity and imagination to go beyond the ordinary and humdrum. This keeps you and your followers excited about what's happening. Great leaders are just ordinary people who do extraordinary things.

♦ You need to be willing and able to do whatever it takes and have the self-discipline to follow through. Example is the best teacher!

♦ You need to exhibit character, courage, and integrity to everyone at all times. No excuses.

♦ You need to be trustworthy by keeping promises, i.e., agreement. No shortcuts allowed. Renegotiation of any agreement is acceptable, if necessary.

♦ You need to develop and maintain a sound body, as much as possible, which contributes to having a sound mind. Exercise and a heart-healthy diet helps you to be fit and gives you the energy to influence others by your excellent example.

♦ You need to be a good communicator by learning to really listen and recognize and respond to both verbal and nonverbal communications.

♦ You need to treat other people like you would have them treat you—with appreciation, respect, fairness, and dignity.

♦ You need to accept responsibility for your actions and your shortcomings, rather than blaming others.

♦ You need to have a forgiving attitude toward yourself and others by giving yourself and them the benefit of the doubt. Otherwise you'll be hurting yourself as you carry around old "baggage." Forgive yourself—for your own peace of mind.

♦ You need a strong belief in the potential of others to see them as they can be—not as they are. This will instill self-confidence and self-esteem in your business or career associates, in your family, with your friends, and with others with whom you have an opportunity to make a positive difference.

♦ You need to treat everyone as an individual who has his or her own wants, needs, and dreams. They may be totally different then yours, but that is what individuality is all about. We all have something unique to give.

♦ You need to always complete important tasks before they become urgent. Stay on top of your game in all areas of your life, delegating as necessary.

How to Be an Effective Communicator

To successfully share an idea, principle or value—with a prospect, customer, spouse, son or daughter, friend, or other people you talk with—you need to be an effective communicator.

Your perception of a given situation, idea, or person and your sincerity, influences your ability to communicate as a leader. Avoid the perception that you are always right. Be humble. No one is *always* right, no matter how intelligent or experienced they may be!

A positive flexible attitude and behavior are essential to create open, clear, and effective communication. Positive flexible attitudes include caring, sincerity, fairness, and being open to new ideas. Positive flexible behavior involves listening to understand, speaking to be understood, and speaking up to people, not down to them. Status, or looking down on someone, has no place in the life of a win-win leader. You might think of a person with status as someone who buys something they can't afford to impress someone they don't like (who probably doesn't care)!

When you communicate, you need to offer your opinion as you see the situation or circumstance. You then need to ask for input and ideas from others. This allows them the opportunity to participate by sharing their unique perspectives and recommendations about the potential solution(s).

Effective communication requires effort. It doesn't just automatically happen. Certain skills are needed and through practice, we can master and perfect those skills. Isn't it true that actors, newscasters, preachers, and politicians often write, then rewrite their scripts? (The secret to writing is rewriting!) Why then, wouldn't we need to practice our communication skills? It just makes sense, doesn't it?

Mutual understanding is a key to effective communication. So we need to mean what we say and say what we mean. Otherwise, our communications will be hindered—to say the least. Listening is also essential in mutual understanding. Unless you hear and understand what the other person is saying, positive and effective communication can't occur. Listening involves patience, openness, and a sincere desire to understand what is being said.

Here's What Can Happen if You Don't Listen to the Prospect

I vividly recall an example of a salesman, who we'll call Joe, who didn't listen to his prospect, a businessman who we'll call George, and almost lost the sale. I had accompanied Joe to propose a large amount of insurance to George so he could fund an agreement to dispose of his business in the event of his death or disability.

After Joe made an effective presentation, he discussed the solution to George's challenge. George then asked a question concerning what appeared to Joe to be a minor detail. However, it apparently was important to George. Instead of allowing George to finish his question, Joe anticipated what he thought George was going to say, interrupted, and gave a response that had nothing to do with the question. George again tried to ask the same question, but again Joe interrupted and offered a response that wasn't relevant.

I could sense the building frustration George was feeling, so I said, "Joe, let's allow George to finish his question." After we both listened to his *real* concern, we were able to respond and satisfy it with ease, and the sale was immediately closed.

The trap of not listening to the full statements or ideas of the prospect, associate, customer or client can damage or be fatal to a relationship. This is true in all our relationships, both personal and professional. You need to listen well to be able to ask meaningful questions and gain more understanding of the other person.

We all need to constantly hone our listening skills and ask appropriate questions to earn the confidence and trust of others. These are key ingredients to building and maintaining healthy successful relationships.

You also earn other people's trust and confidence by your honesty, integrity, and understanding. They need to know you care about them, their needs, and wants. And listening attentively lays the foundation for a quality relationship. You can have many fine values and characteristics, and be as "pure as the driven snow," as some say, but if you don't listen to what others have to say, none of that will matter.

Poor listening skills will get you into trouble, time and time again. You gain and sustain another's confidence and trust because of your ability to be consistent in your interest in them as well as in your vision and actions. You need to sincerely walk your talk in the process and show others, by your outstanding example, how to listen well.

How Well Do You Understand Nonverbal Communication?

As we covered briefly earlier, a leader needs to be knowledgeable in nonverbal as well as verbal messages. Body position, body movements, and voice modulation (tones) are significant in understanding nonverbal communication.

We all have and use nonverbal methods to convey our feelings and thoughts, whether we're consciously doing it or not. Here are a few of them.

- ◆ Your eyes, next to your voice, are your most powerful sources of communication. Eye contact is crucial when speaking with someone because it conveys interest, sincerity, confidence, concern, and trust. Lack of eye contact expresses a lack of interest or confidence and self-esteem. "Do they really mean what they are saying?"
- ◆ Remember your firm handshake with eye contact. They communicate confidence and interest.
- ◆ Your face is usually the most expressive part of your body (including those with a deadpan look!), and your facial expressions can communicate your feelings rather dramatically. It's highly likely that through your facial expressions you vividly reveal your feelings of interest, excitement, surprise, joy, anger, fear, sadness, or disinterest.
- ◆ A genuine smile conveys your warm feelings, but a forced smile is quickly seen as false. Just showing your teeth isn't enough! Your entire face needs to break out in a smile (with your lips open) to reflect interest and gladness. Your eyes seem to sparkle; there is no frown; and your mouth opens, widens and curves upward on both sides.

   You may be laughing at my detailed description right now. Yet, have you seen people whose face is so determinedly set in a frown or a look of boredom that you expect their face to crack if they "shocked" it with a smile? Or those who flash their teeth because they believe they must, rather than give a sincere smile? *That* is why I describe the act of smiling so thoroughly, especially for those who haven't conquered the art!

♦ The ability to read posture allows you to determine how another person feels (and what you're projecting if you do the same thing). When they stand straight with relaxed but squared shoulders, perhaps with their hands positioned behind their back, there is a sign of confidence and strength. If they're seated and leaning forward, it's often a sign of interest and confidence. If shoulders droop, it is usually a sign of self-consciousness, guilt, fear, or lack of confidence and self-esteem.

Remember, when someone stands or sits with arms folded across their chest, it usually indicates lack of interest and a closed mind, even if it's done just because they're cold or tired. So it's best to avoid the closed look.

♦ People signal their thoughts by various gestures. For example, in the U.S., thumbs up indicates a job well done; a "high five" with outstretched palms is for victory or a good deed; a clenched fist raised in the air can be a sign of cheering someone on or a motivational function of being fired up; and a raised index finger signifies the person is number one. (Be careful if you travel internationally. An innocent, positive gesture in one country could be a rude gesture elsewhere! Learn about the culture, or you could get yourself in trouble!)

♦ Many of us have nonverbal habits we don't realize that may be distracting and indicate nervousness. Things such as constant jingling of the coins in our pocket, repeated clicking of a ballpoint pen, picking or biting our nails, "cracking" our knuckles, constantly tapping a pencil or fingers on the desk or table, wringing or clenching our hands, and rubbing our neck can be annoying.

♦ In the U.S., a light touch on the head, shoulder, or a pat on the back can be used to convey positive feelings of "I like you," and/or "congratulations on your accomplishment." Again, this could vary from one country to another.

Review your own nonverbal cues and fine-tune them so you are supporting rather than taking away from the effectiveness of your communications. Always be alert to the nonverbal signals from others so you can respond to their needs and concerns appropriately. It can pay big dividends!

Are You Planning for Success?

Planning is indispensable for business people. They need to make effective use of their time to maximize their results. The key, however, is not just planning but *flexible* planning.

If plans have no flexibility, you may be spending your valuable time "spinning your wheels," because something went wrong, i.e., not according to your plan. "What can go wrong with a well developed plan?" you may be asking yourself. Someone cancels his or her appointment at the last minute. Perhaps a prospect or customer forgets they have an appointment with you. So they've made other plans and aren't there when you arrive. Or you have a situation requiring your immediate attention that comes up in your family or business that precludes following your plan.

Flexible planning helps you work around the unexpected. From your past experiences, you know such things are bound to happen. Very seldom do things go *exactly* as planned. It's impossible to anticipate and plan for every possible challenge that might present itself! Therefore, when things don't go as expected, don't let it bother you. Forget it, pick up the pieces, and move on.

Do you want to maximize your productivity? Then you need to make more appointments than you can keep. If an appointment is canceled or postponed, as it could well be, you're more likely to have another person to fill in that spot in your schedule. If both are available, i.e., you're double booked, you can always reschedule. This is effectively a form of posturization. You're letting that person know you are busy and in demand; you're "pushing them back." This puts you in control, rather than a prospect or customer who has canceled. If you're running late because of overbooking, a telephone call to your next appointment is courteous and will be understood. Once again, it's a push back. Besides which, people respect and like to do business with busy people. They are known to be the ones who get things done.

More Tips on Achieving Top-Notch Sales Performance

Bill Gove, a well-known sales consultant, says, "Selling is not talking someone into doing something he doesn't want to do. People like to buy. Selling then, is making it easy for him to do what he enjoys doing."

He continues, "Sure the professional salesman gives the prospect reasons why it's better to buy now than it is to delay, but he makes sure that the reasons he gives are the prospect's *not* his."

Gove gives us three things salespeople and those building an organization of business associates do:

1. Build growing relationships. Establish yourself as a problem solver by understanding the prospect's needs and wants. Keep your presentation on track and respect their time and opinions.
2. Make it easy for the prospect to act by helping them arrive at their own decision. Reassure them that their decision is rational by direct and indirect suggestion.
3. Help them recognize and remove any obstacles that stand in the way, such as delay (I'll think it over); time or money (I don't have any time or money); or resistance to change (I'm satisfied with the way things are).

The Story of The Hot Dog Vendor

This story illustrates a positive and a negative approach to marketing:

There was a man who lived by the side of the road who sold very good hot dogs. He put up signs along the highway and advertised in the newspaper telling how tasty they were.

He stood on the side of the road and cried out, "Buy a hot dog?" And people stopped and bought. He increased his meat and bun orders. He bought a bigger stand to take care of his growing business.

He finally got his son, who was home from college, to help him out. But then something happened. His son said, "Father, haven't you been listening to the radio and watching TV? There is a big depression, and the foreign situation is terrible. And the domestic situation is even worse."

Whereupon the father thought, "Well, my son has been to college, and he ought to know." So the father cut down on his meat and bun order, took down his signs, canceled his newspaper ads, and no longer bothered to stand out on the highway to sell his hot dogs. His sales fell almost overnight.

"You're right, son," the father said to the boy. "We certainly are in the middle of a great depression."

Most of the "Apples in the Barrel" Are Good

Some people don't want to be in sales or their own business because they have been unsuccessful at it in the past or perhaps know someone who did not do well at it. That suggests they have been selling everything under the sun, i.e., except themselves, and may not have cared enough about their prospects.

A Louis Harris survey taken in the 50's indicates that among the top three pet peeves of most Americans is, "the fast talking salesman." If you live outside the U.S., that may also be true

The more you think about this, it's likely you can point to most professions and find a few who dishonor the reputation of many. For example, you may know of religious leaders who have come under scrutiny for their out of line behavior, lawyers whose practices are illegal or questionable at best, "physicians" who are unlicensed, or politicians who abuse their power. These few are not a true reflection on the many in their particular line of work who are straightforward and honest. Most of the "apples in the barrel" are good!

The profession of selling, or having your own independent business, deserves a great reputation because of the good it does for so many. Where would we be without sales or business? We'd have no commerce, would we? Businesses and salespeople often provide good products and services that could help people in many different ways.

But even more important, those who invest in their own personal development as a part of their on going training and education almost always grow and become better people. They need to follow the fundamentals of good salesmanship (sharemanship) and leadership. This means understanding and caring about people, their prospects, customers, and business associates. It also means understanding their products, services, and ideas and how they can best serve others.

In addition to this, they also need to constantly treat others in such a way that they earn their trust and are known for their integrity. As more and more salespeople meet these standards, they can improve their standing in the community of professionals and with the general public.

Salespeople succeed or fail in direct relation to their volume. They can't get by on just their credibility and reputation without consistent, productive effort. They are not paid by the number of hours worked; they are paid for results. Results and results only pay their bills and build their lifestyle to new levels.

Being in sales or in your own independent business offers you an opportunity to earn an income that relates directly to *your* talent, effort, and attitude. To take full advantage of this almost limitless opportunity for tremendous success, you need to be fully prepared to open the door when opportunity knocks. Always be looking for potential buyers. And if you're building an organization of associates, always be on the lookout for sharp, ambitious people who want more out of life. Be ready for when the "right" person comes along.

Chapter Six

A Positive Attitude Prepares You For Opportunity

"Opportunity is missed by most people because it is dressed in overalls and looks like work."
Thomas A. Edison

Opportunity Is an Inside Job

Ralph Waldo Emerson, American poet, lecturer, and essayist, wrote, "Real opportunity lies within a person, not outside. What lies behind you and what lies before you are tiny matters compared to what lies within you."

People in need of and perhaps looking for excellent products, services, and opportunities are everywhere. You just need to keep meeting and talking with people, "going through the numbers," as they say, to find them. You need to get and stay plugged into a continuing education and motivational program, doing whatever it takes to have a positive attitude as you keep persisting in the process.

The more people you meet and help, the closer you're likely to get to your dreams and goals. If you have a negative attitude, prospects may appear as problems rather than opportunities. You need to recognize and use your best ideas to make the most of the chance you have to build your career or business with those who present themselves to you everywhere, every day. You may have a fleeting couple of minutes with another person, who could turn out to be the best prospect you've ever had. Take advantage of these sometimes golden opportunities you have to cultivate a new win-win relationship. Remember, luck is when opportunity and preparedness meet.

Blocked by their own perceived limitations, some people don't look at people as they can be—perhaps an excellent customer or associate. Alertness to such possibilities can help you break through any fear and take advantage of the moment you're given to strike up a conversation that could lead to a mutually beneficial outcome.

And remember, limitations are *self-imposed.* Until they are recognized for what they are—falsehoods—and they are removed, it won't be possible for you to see and use the many opportunities for meeting new people who present themselves every day. This is part of moving ahead with focus and commitment. Utilizing these often-golden opportunities to reach out to others will make the journey to your dream more exciting and can also shorten the time for your goals to materialize.

What Could Be Holding *You* Back?

Are you moving on as quickly as you'd like? Most people would answer no to this question. Surely success is a process and takes time. Yet most of us could shorten the process by pinpointing and eliminating any false beliefs we may have adopted that have caused us to put the brakes on our progress. Here's a list of false beliefs that may be hampering the growth you desire—along with some ideas to help you take action:

♦ *Believing that a lack of a college degree or other education is preventing you from succeeding.* Many people are self-taught—they weren't officially educated in their business or career. Formal education is not the key to success.

♦ *Believing that you need a lot of money to start a new business.* Many businesses can be started at home with minimal expense. Time is often your major investment here—sweat equity and investing in your continuing education program—which is essential.

♦ *Believing that you can't acquire the necessary knowledge or skills to succeed, particularly in dealing with people.* Be encouraged! You can always learn what you need to know. Other people do it and you can too.

Learning to understand people and skillfully work with them can be done through continuing education and experience. Some of the best lessons can be learned by observing others' behaviors, how they affect you, and being determined to *not* do to others what's affected you negatively!

♦ *Believing you don't need an action plan.* The fact is—you do! Get with your leader or mentor if you need help to make one.

♦ *Believing that you don't have time.* We all have 24 hours a day. And, while you can't control time, but you can manage your activities to make the most profitable use of your time.

♦ *Believing your self-confidence and self-esteem are low.* Know you're not alone! Fortunately, action cures fear. If you don't already have a leader or mentor, find one who believes in you and will work with you.

♦ *Believing negative experiences hold you back.* Practice asking yourself, "What can I learn from this? (And then answering!)

♦ *Believing that you can't have a more positive attitude.* We all need to monitor our attitude and upgrade it, as necessary, throughout each day. Everyone has room for improvement.

After carefully reviewing any limitations you may have been imposing on yourself, along with the suggestions for change, take them one at a time and remove them from your mind. Eliminate their holding back effect on your business or profession. This is challenging and takes time to achieve. But it's worth it!

You may need to change your career and increase your perseverance and willingness to change your thinking or goals to accomplish what you really want to do. Eventually, as you continue to work at it, you can remove all of these self-imposed limitations. You'll just need to monitor yourself to be sure you stay on track, like all of us need to do. You'll then be on your way to a more rewarding and satisfying life.

Change Your Habits and You'll Change Your Life

Are some of your habits slowing you down or deterring you from making the progress you'd like to make? People are creatures of habit. We form habits that help form our future.

Therefore, to win, we need to continually eliminate any destructive habits and, through constant-spaced repetition, form new constructive ones. As mentioned in an earlier chapter, it takes approximately 21 days to change a habit—that's all! Through consistent effort and dedication for this period, we can make the change. If you find yourself falling back to any old unwanted habit, you need to start the 21-day period over again.

It's likely many of your habits have been with you for a long time. Therefore, changing them will require persistence. It will take your conviction that you honestly want new results enough to put forth the effort to change and your dedication to the change process.

Some of your habits could be getting in the way and actually slowing down or obstructing your realization of your dream, your big idea, or your goal. You need to recognize those habits that you need to change so you can increase your progress. Get a piece of paper and a pen. Take time now to think quietly and seriously, then write down the habits you want to change.

Here are some examples of habits that may need changing: allowing unimportant details to get in the way of your priorities, watching to much television, not allowing time each day for your personal development, lack of organization in your daily work, and a lack of flexible planning. Do any of these success-defeating habits apply to you? Perhaps one or more of these, and many others that you may be guilty of, need to be identified, listed, and changed as quickly as possible. Attack first those habits that are obstructing your progress the most. The sooner you start, the better!

Use Your Imagination

Imagination is another factor that opens doors to a world of wonderful opportunities. Use your ability to think and create and put to use your powerful force of imagination. Whatever you can think of and sincerely believe you can do, you can make it a reality! As Ralph Waldo Emerson once said, "A feeble man can see the farms that are fenced and tilled, the houses that are built. The strong man sees the possible houses and farms (that aren't built). His eye makes estates as fast as the sun breeds clouds."

Because of your busy and perhaps sometimes uncertain schedule, you may not take time to pause and think. Make an appointment with yourself at least once a week, better yet once a day, to make your significant imagination process work. This can be some of the most productive and enjoyable time in your entire schedule. It'll give you more of a sense of control over your progress and help keep you on track toward your dreams and goals.

When you invest the time needed to plant seeds in your mind and allow your creative juices to flow, your imagination will take over. You'll open doors to new exciting ideas that will surely lead to creative opportunities for you, your family, and in your business or profession. Sit down and dream of what can be an open-minded brainstorm to discover new ways of thinking about a challenge and creative solutions. Do this with your leader or mentor, someone who cares about and supports you.

How Can You Serve Others?

Take full advantage of opportunities to serve other people. Most everyone provides a service of some kind. It may be offering a tangible product or a so-called intangible service or opportunity. Some examples of intangible services performed by a person with a positive attitude include a housewife and mother providing homemaking services to her family, a courteous salesperson selling a lawn care service, a pleasant bus driver who's consistently on time, friendly administrative assistants serving other divisions of their company without being asked.

Other examples could include: a caring mentor or leader counseling someone and helping them with their action plan, and the compassionate independent businessperson who is offering someone an opportunity to develop themselves and improve their life or excellent products and services that can save them time and money.

You Are Equally Compensated for the Service You Render

The rewards you receive—emotional, material, or something else—will be in exact proportion to the type, amount, and quality of the product, service, or opportunity you provide. A fine product, marketed properly, will bring a higher price and greater satisfaction than an inferior product or service. Being truly supportive, sincere, and providing prompt thorough service and assistance helps you create confidence and repeat business. You'll also have the internal satisfaction that you've done your very best to help others with what you're sharing. The financial bottom line to all this is basically this: when you want more income, you need to serve and assist more people!

Appreciating Change

It has often been said, "There is opportunity in change." Think of the enormous changes that have taken place in the world in the last 5years, the last 25 years, and the last 100 years. If no one had boldly stepped forth to take advantage of the tremendous changes that created virtually unlimited opportunities, where would we all be?

Where would we be without electricity, telephones, computers, e-mail, automobiles, jet aircraft, advanced medical technology, or without most of the luxuries that many of us expect and enjoy every day without even thinking about it? What if no one bothered to invent and manufacture these and countless other things that make our lives easier?

The Ring of Freedom

One of the privileges you have today that was not as evident in past years is the freedom you enjoy. This is particularly true for those of us living in the U.S. and other free countries throughout the world. As you're well aware, your freedoms did not come easily or without sacrifice. Among others, you have the freedom to decide what you want to do with the rest of your life, the freedom to be an entrepreneur, the freedom to work for someone else, and the freedom to change your life—from this day forward.

Former President of the U. S. Dwight D. Eisenhower once said in a speech, "Freedom in our democracy is, in simple terms, an opportunity for a man to develop self-discipline."

A phrase bears repeating here—*if it is to be, it's up to me!*

It's only natural for a group of people to look at the same opportunity from a different viewpoint. Some will look at it in a positive way, while others will look at it in a negative way. There are undoubtedly a few that might not even know an opportunity is present. You are the sole judge of what your freedom or any other opportunity means to you. It's important that you are ready, mentally and physically, to recognize and take full advantage of every one that comes along.

For example, when a person comes along you'd like to introduce yourself to, be aware and poised to grasp that often-fleeting couple of moments that you have to meet them. When opportunity knocks, be prepared to open the door. When you meet someone new, reach out your hand and say, "Hi, my name is _____. What's yours?" or something else, as appropriate.

Surveys indicate that the great majority of people seem to look at where they are as being as far as they'll go. They don't see the forest for the trees. They don't see the opportunities that are right in front of them. It's no wonder that many people are emotionally dead before they even hit their 30's. Why is this? What happens to their hope?

They need to realize how greatly expanding and dynamic industries need and seek uncommon people to share in their growth. For example, many cutting edge companies are expanding globally through the Internet and are able to help many more people with their products, services, and opportunities much more quickly.

Some companies on the grow often will richly reward people of vision who prepare themselves to move up as their industry grows larger and larger. (An aside: The companies will lose out, however, if they fail to remember that first and foremost their business is a people business. People are their most important resource, both in-house as well as customers and other associates, i.e., vendors, distributors, and such. So as a leader or an aspiring leader, keep this concept in mind as you build your business or career.)

Opportunities abound for those who search for them. Unfortunately there are many people who feel their government, family, or employer owes them a living. You probably learned a long time ago that, "you don't get something for nothing." You need to earn it the old-fashioned way by working for it. No matter how often opportunity knocks, we need to put forth the necessary effort to make it work for us.

Some say, "But I can't find a job; there's no work available." Just look at the help wanted ads of any major newspaper and you'll find hundreds and, in some cases, thousands of opportunities for those who are really looking for work. And up to 10 percent of the ads are for sales and marketing positions. Look for something you'll enjoy doing. People who just blindly take a job because it pays well or simply because there's an opening somewhere end up regretting they weren't more careful in their approach to job hunting.

The point is that in all economic situations, upturns or downturns, there is opportunity everywhere for those willing to be flexible and positive about the future. True, you may have to change your lifestyle and career direction and make sacrifices, but you can move forward toward your dreams and goals from wherever you are. About 70 percent of people don't like their jobs. If everyone would take full advantage of the opportunities out there and find a job or a business they love, imagine what a happier world this would be!

Here's a list of five characteristics of successful people, with some key ideas for taking full advantage of your opportunities:

1. Self-Discipline
◆ Manage your time and activities for maximum effectiveness. Time is money.
◆ Plan your work and work your plan.
◆ Put off until tomorrow only what doesn't need to be done today.

♦ Keep records. In order to know where you are going, you need to know where you've been.

♦ You can only succeed in your business or career when you have self-discipline. Focus on disciplining yourself in one key area at a time and you'll be on your way.

2. Drive

♦ Get involved in your industry's concerns. Be an advocate for doing what's best for everyone in the short and long run.

♦ Get up and go. Get started NOW!

♦ Prepare to pay the price, make sacrifices, and do whatever it takes.

3. Emotional Stability

♦ Overcome any obstacle you can and learn to live with and work around any situations that can't be changed.

♦ Always look for the positive side of what may appear to be a negative experience.

♦ Develop mental toughness. Have a tough skin and a warm heart. "When the going gets tough, the tough get going." Conversely, as noted author and speaker Jay Rifenbary says, "When the going gets tough, the weak blame." Be a resilient, responsible person!

4. Knowledge

♦ Confidence is essential and will grow with your continuing education program of books, tapes, and seminars.

♦ Power results from your ability to communicate your knowledge to prospects, friends, family, associates, and others you deal with.

♦ *Leaders are readers,* and a person who knows grows. They read 15 to 30 minutes a day from a positive book for long-term personal growth.

♦ Professionalism is the result of competence in your field.

♦ Retrain if needed.

5. Belief

♦ Maintain the conviction that what you're doing is right for you, your family, and your business or career.

♦ Anything is possible when you believe in yourself.
♦ Have confidence in your products, services, opportunities, company, and leadership.
♦ Be humble and thankful for your family, your business or career, and your blessings.

Of course, the most important characteristic for success, and taking full advantage of your opportunities, is a positive mental attitude.

Chapter Seven

Decision, Commitment, Dedication, Conviction, and Persistence

"Your own resolution to success is more important than any other one thing."
Abraham Lincoln

Have You Been Keeping Your Promises?

Talk is cheap, but performance is king. People will often make promises to others or themselves with no real intention to follow through to a successful conclusion. Such people fail to use their time and talent to really go for their goals and dreams. They often lead fairly empty lives, not realizing what's missing. This situation is extremely common and may even apply to you.

Broken promises and the disappointment that results can lead to ill feelings among friends, family, and business associates. If we've broken our promises, it may also lead them to have a negative attitude about our intentions. There's no excuse for this behavior. When we say we're going to *do* something, we need to *do* it! Don't you agree?

Decide and You're Half Done

There are two ways to get to the top of an oak tree. You can sit on an acorn and wait for the tree to grow, or you can start climbing—now! You don't wait until the perfect time (there is none!) and you don't make excuses. You make the decision to move on and to do whatever it takes. It's the first step toward the progressive realization of your dreams and goals.

Many people have not taken the lead in their own lives. They more or less live in a reaction mode, doing what they believe others expect them to do and following orders. They're often in a non-thinking state, depending on the wants and whims of others. This isn't a crime but it certainly doesn't lead to success and happiness from a life of contribution that's for sure.

When people realize no one else will pursue their dreams and goals for them, they're just not going to happen—plain and simple. Other people are generally too self-involved to care, except your leader or mentor and hopefully your spouse if you're married. Some people have a very supportive loving family and friends. But even if you do, you are still in the driver's seat when it comes to your dreams and goals. It's up to you to make that quality decision about what may have been in your heart for a long time. No one else can make that decision for you. They're responsible only for their *own* dreams and goals, not yours!

How Committed and Dedicated Are You?

Vince Lombardi, former college and professional football coach, once said, "The quality of a man's life is in direct proportion to his commitment to excellence, regardless of his chosen field."

There are many definitions of commitment. The most significant, in reference to improving the quality of your life, is a promise or a pledge to do something.

Once you've made a quality decision, commit yourself completely to making it happen. Dedicate yourself to getting the job done and to achieving your dream or goal. Your dedication and effort express your devotion after you've made the decision to do it!

Here's one of my favorite funny stories about dedication: A man and his wife were playing golf during a hot, humid afternoon. On the tenth fairway she stepped in a gopher hole and broke her leg.

Since it was late and there was no one available to assist them, he carried her and both sets of clubs back to the clubhouse to obtain medical care. Can you picture this slight 5'6" 150 pound man carrying his 5'7" 130-pound wife and their two golf bags?

Everyone was astounded and asked how he could have carried her so far. "What a feat," they said. His response was, "It really wasn't that bad. The hardest part was putting her down and picking her up again after each shot on the last eight holes." That's dedication!

Of course, this man's dedication was to the wrong thing. The best thing he could've done would have been to stop playing golf and attend to the needs of his wife. So be sure *you're* dedicated to the *right* thing!

One of the most important realities I learned during my leadership career was, "People generally are more dedicated to and work harder for the things money won't buy." It will not buy honor, influence, recognition, a reputation for integrity, or the true satisfaction of a job well done. Only hard and smart work, commitment, dedication, and persistence will give you these rewards. Think about it.

Persist and Persist, Then Persist Some More!

Former U.S. President Calvin Coolidge once said, "Nothing in the world can take the place of persistence. Talent will not; nothing is more common than unsuccessful men with talent. Genius will not; unrewarded genius is almost a proverb. Education will not; the world is full of educated derelicts. Persistence and determination alone are omnipotent. The slogan 'Press On' has solved and always will solve the problems of the human race."

Even if you feel like quitting, don't! People who have made a firm decision, are committed and dedicated to it, and persevere—no matter what the obstacles are—win. Take some deep breaths and keep going. Be dogged in pursuit of your dreams and goals. If you won't, who will? If you don't pursue them now, then when will you? If what you're doing now won't enable you to make your dreams come true, then what will?

Duplicate the achievers. Do whatever it takes, however many times, to make what you want a reality. As Helen Keller once said, "Be of good cheer. Do not think of today's failures, but of the success that may come tomorrow. You have set yourself a (challenging) task, but you will succeed if you persevere; and you will find a joy in overcoming obstacles. Remember, no effort that we make to attain something beautiful is ever lost."

Do You Have Conviction?

Conviction is also essential to successfully achieve your goals and dreams. It's a strong belief in what you're doing, being convinced that it is the right thing for you to do. You need conviction to complete all tasks associated with achieving your dreams and goals, especially the mundane ones. Your experience, education, and environment influence the strength of your conviction. In many cases, you may need to be re-educated. This is where your continuing education program of books, tapes, and seminars comes in handy. It can help you become a stronger believer in the value of what you're doing.

The Power of Conviction

As a person who helps others, you're also a creator. Where there is despair, you can create opportunity and hope; where there is suffering, you can create comfort; where there is loss, you can create profit; where there are tears, you can create smiles. Isn't this basically the whole story of being a person who helps others?

Do you believe you can and perhaps have created such things as these, or at least did your very best to do so? Is your conviction strong enough to carry you from the disappointment of not achieving a goal as soon as you had planned to the happiness of achieving it when you actually do? This is simply the Power of Conviction, a power every successful person needs to own.

Do you honestly believe what you're doing offers the best solution to the challenges of your customers, prospects, and associates? Do you honestly believe it will help them improve their quality of life through your products(s), service(s), and opportunity? Are you convinced that what you do is significant and needed to help people live the life they want? Do you believe that what you have to share gives people hope for a better life themselves, and perhaps even a wonderful way to make a difference in other people's lives as well?

If you truly believe in what you're doing, than I suggest you tell everyone you meet about it. If you are doubtful or uncertain, I suggest you reexamine your beliefs. How is your power of conviction? Will it help carry you to the finish line of each of your dreams and goals?

Share What You've Been Given

This statement relates to everyone. We're all salespeople of sorts. We need to eliminate the old idea that sales is an intrusion to push something people don't want or need and probably can't afford. However, instead of calling it sales, call it sharing. Many of us share our lives in marriage. We share understanding and ideals with our children. We share friendship and loyalty with our friends. We share abilities and efforts in our business or profession to serve others. We share our values and opinions when we engage in community activities. We share our compassion and ideas to help others have happier, more productive lives.

Where would the world be if the vast number of innovators and inventors had not been able to share their ideas or products with others? Obviously, some scoff at, ridicule, and put down a new idea or invention. Think about this: where would we all be if the world were run by those who have said, "It can't be done"?

Remember, there are three kinds of people: those who make things happen; those who watch things happen; and those who wonder what happened. If you're not already, you can be the person who *makes* things happen. You first need to decide you want to make them happen badly enough. You often need to be fed up with how things are in your life, in one or more areas, or very excited about making a positive change. These emotions help to fuel your mind and heart to get you to take action.

Decision, commitment, dedication, conviction, and persistence are some of the key ingredients that differentiate between mediocrity and greatness. Adopt those characteristics and habits in your life, and you can achieve whatever you truly desire. The ball is in your court.

Make good things happen in your life by sharing what you have to offer with others. If you don't do it you'll never know what would have happened if you had done it! Now, doesn't that make you think.

Chapter Eight

High Performance Use
Of Your Time

"One can never consent to creep when one feels an impulse to soar."
Helen Keller

Be Productive, Not Just Busy

To continue your development as a leader, you need to use your time wisely, positively and effectively. Be productive, not just busy!

I recall a situation that caused my insurance agency's regional vice-president to step in and confront me several years ago. First of all, I had scheduled a vacation during the first two weeks of November. I was also selected to represent our company at an industry-wide training council meeting in Washington, D.C., during the fourth week in November. Secondly, our agency was in contention for a company leadership award based on our year-end results. It was to be presented at the company's International Convention early the next year.

Learning of my out-of-the-office commitments scheduled for that November, he surprised me by saying, "Tom, don't you realize you'll be out of the office for three weeks next month? I suggest you change your plans so the office will continue to be productive during this crucial part of the year."

After a few seconds of thought, I responded, "I can appreciate your concern for my office; however, if I felt that my absence would adversely affect our production, I would surely change my plans." I continued, "I am an effective leader, and I have made specific plans for the continued production of my staff while I'm away. I would be admitting I was not an effective leader if I felt I needed to be in the office for the staff to be productive."

What was the outcome? As a result of our discussion, he didn't force me to change my plans. That November my office had the highest production month in the history of the agency. We exceeded our goals.

Make Each Day Count

Time keeps ticking away, regardless of whether you're on-track or off-track in pursuing your dreams and goals. You need to make productive use of your time to achieve what you want in life. To keep doing the same things with your time, while expecting different results, is simply fooling yourself.

Most people believe it's a lack of time that's limiting their income and keeping them from reaching their goals. But we all have 24 hours a day. The difference between whether we succeed or fail is how we use, or rather *invest* our time. If we use our time ineffectively, we not only keep missing the mark with our goals, but it also adds considerable stress and confusion to our lives. Are those the results *you* want? I seriously doubt it!

Smart investment of your time is central to your success. To keep it simple and specific, this means you're getting things done. I stress getting the *right* things done not just anything done. Since time is your most precious asset, you need to invest it productively and effectively, otherwise it just disappears and you have little, if anything to show for it. Sure, things will have changed—you're older, and so is everyone else who is still alive.

The question will be: "Are you better off?" If you're not, it's most likely because you used your time in such a way that didn't result in reaching your goals. You were probably busy, but not very productive.

You cannot control time; it just is! Seconds tick into minutes, hours, days, weeks, months, years, decades, and centuries. High performance *use of time* is probably the most important thing in developing a successful business or career, and a successful life. Consider it this way. A successful life is simply a lot of successful days put together. To reach your goals in as little time as possible, you need to *make each day count.*

Each day consists of a series of events and tasks. Some are important to your success, while others are not. The success of each day depends on the results of the events and the completion of each task that you need to do that day.

How Can You Become More Effective?

To improve the effective use of your personal and business time, start by reviewing yesterday's events. Begin with the moment you got up until you went to bed. Recall and picture the activities that filled your day. List each activity and the time you spent on it. Include the time showering, eating, dressing, traveling to and from work, what you did at work, what you did with your secondary income generator, i.e., job or business, family time, relaxing, and any other activities you were involved in.

After you've compiled your list from yesterday, continue doing it each day for seven days to get a more complete picture of all your activities and the time you spent doing them. When the seven days are over, review all your lists and determine which activities are essential for the accomplishment of your goals and which aren't.

Could you have spent less time on unimportant things, such as watching TV or playing with your computer, when that time could have been used more profitably toward your goal? How could you eliminate a few unnecessary activities or ones that can be delegated to your family, for example? Arrange your activities so that you personally do only those things you cannot delegate and those that move you forward.

You may have fallen into the habit of doing things other people (besides a boss asking you to do something appropriate to your job) want you to do, even though doing these activities keeps you from pursuing your goals. Instead of being goal-achieving, they are often people pleasing or perhaps procrastinating what they may be uncomfortable about or don't feel like doing. What might you have done today that others wanted you to do that weren't goal achieving or that you did to procrastinate doing what you need to do? People who get the essential goal-oriented things done and make things happen say no to others and themselves, regarding committing themselves to doing things that would get them off-track.

For example, if they're asked to coach little league baseball and they need to do work on business-oriented activities some evenings, they politely decline and perhaps recommend another parent they know to do it. Remember that being successful isn't a popularity contest. You can't please everyone all the time, so you might as well please yourself!

Getting the right things done each day not only makes you a positive user (investor) of your time, but it will also move you more quickly towards your goals and dreams. You might be in the habit of doing only things you enjoy or perhaps maintenance-type activities. You may not have realized it, but these habits can seriously delay your accomplishment of your overall dream. Do the things that keep you on your journey of success. Delay gratification short-term, do what's necessary to achieve your goals, and you'll have your dream long-term.

The following article, author unknown, illustrates the reason why productive use of your time is so important:

Getting Things Done

"The world has always cried for men and women who can
get things done, for people who are self-starters,
who see a task through to its finish.
It isn't how much you know, but what you get done that the
world rewards and remembers.

More people are held back from success because they
don't know how to get things done—
more than for any other single reason.
The biggest handicap to success is not a lack of brains, nor
a lack of character or willingness.

It is weakness in getting things done.
This large group of people know what to do, and almost do
it on time. They almost attain the next level. They almost
become leaders. They may miss by only a minute or an inch,
but they do miss until they learn how
to gain that minute or inch for themselves.

The almosts are not lazy. Often they are busier than the
effective few. They putter around fuzzily all day long and half
the night, though they fail to accomplish much.
They are held back by indecision, lack of organization in
their work, and dwelling on minor details.

They are swirled around in circles and get nowhere. They
may chart a straight course, but they don't then stick to it.
We don't need to work harder, we need to work smarter.
We need to learn to make each day count.

It is the producers who raise the world's standard of
living. It is the producers who win the big share
of the world's rewards. The producers are those people who
have formed the habit of getting things done, who will not
permit the 'almosts' to get them off course."

Six Tips on Everyday Planning for Effectively Using Your Time.

1. Get yourself a day planner. For example, the Franklin Covey Company offers several styles and sizes—even a pocket size. Take it with you everywhere you go. Follow the simple instructions provided with the day planner, if any. Until you get a planner, carry a small date book, note pad, or three by five index cards in your pocket or purse to jot down things that need to be done.
2. The best way to make progress is to schedule your activities into your planner. Plan tomorrow's activities tonight. Don't wait for tomorrow morning to set your plans and schedule for the day.
3. Plan your day tightly. Schedule enough things to keep you productive and moving in the right direction.

4. Schedule your outgoing telephone calls so they can be done in one sitting. Have all the numbers ready to streamline your calling. Most planners have an address and phone number section in the back.

5. Plan productive things you can read, work on, or think about while you're waiting for an appointment. Listen to motivational tapes while driving, and turn your car into a university on wheels. Also keep a positive book handy for any other idle moments that crop up.

6. Almost everyone goes to bed at different hours, but as a rule, they rise at the same hour each morning. Set your alarm one hour earlier. You will gain nine 40-hour weeks a year!

Here's a poem (author unknown) that touches on getting started:

Start It

"When there is anything to do, I start.
Don't look at a thing; start it.
Don't imagine that it is too difficult; start it.
Don't put it off for a day; start it.

Don't look for someone else to do it; start it.
Don't pretend that you must think it over; start it.
Don't start half-heartedly, put everything that
you can muster into your start."

Effective, high-performance use of your time is necessary to become the leader you want to be and build a successful career or business. You'll be better able to reach your goals and dreams, both personally and professionally. This will then give you the time you need to do those things you want to do for a full and substantial life for you and your family, as well as in your business or profession.

Chapter Nine

Does Luck Have An Impact On Leadership?

*"I'm a great believer in luck, and I find the harder I work
the more I have it."*
Thomas Jefferson

What Does Luck Have to Do With It?

Webster's New Collegiate Dictionary describes luck as "that which happens to one seemingly by chance, fate, or fortune. Good luck is favorable fortune."

The definition of lucky is—"favored by luck; fortunate. Producing or resulting in good, by chance or unexpectedly; favorable; fortunate. Lucky implies success by chance rather than as the result of merit."

I've been told that I've been lucky in my business and personal life. I always agree, because good fortune has smiled in many ways at my family and me. Overall, we have enjoyed good health (a positive attitude has a great deal of impact on this) and an abundance of happiness. I believe, however, that my luck has been the result of a definition considerably different than the dictionary's definition. I would define luck in the following manner:

- ◆ **L** is for Leadership
- ◆ **U** is for Understanding

- ◆ **C** is for Capabilities and Communication
- ◆ **K** is for Knowledge

Think about this. You can and do, by and large, make your own "luck." Now, let's examine these four ingredients.

Leadership

Leaders have vision, a sense of purpose, and a mission to guide them. They know the difference between efficiency and effectiveness. Efficiency is doing things right, and effectiveness is doing the right thing. There is a significant difference, isn't there?

Leaders are proactive rather than reactive, and they make things happen. Leaders lead by their behavior and actions, not just by what they say. They walk their talk and lead by example. They get people to accomplish things they wouldn't do otherwise.

Understanding

Leaders point the way for others to follow, not from obedience but from understanding. They listen with empathy because they have an understanding of people and have often experienced similar challenges. My mentor once remarked, "People knowledge (understanding and skill with people) is 95 percent essential (of what's needed) to achieve success, whereas product knowledge is only 5 percent essential (of what's needed)."

Think about it. When you understand people, their frailties and wants, you can be an effective leader and help to make your own luck.

All people have basic human wants and frailties, i.e., tendencies. An in-depth understanding of these wants and frailties are needed to better understand why people act or react as they do in a given situation.

Basic Human Desires

To best understand people, you need to know what the basic human desires are. Here's a list of eight:

♦ **Desire for belonging.** You want to feel as if you are needed and wanted by certain others you associate with. This was probably most evident when you were a teenager, if you conformed like many teenagers do. As you've matured, you've probably noticed that you have a better sense of who you are and what you can do. It's likely you have broadened and perhaps changed the scope of people with whom you desire a feeling of belonging.

♦ **Desire for love and affection.** Unconditional love of self and others is the most powerful positive emotion. It supports your self-esteem (self-respect) and dramatically enhances your ability to effectively and compassionately communicate with yourself (self-talk) and others. A lack of unconditional love and understanding is largely responsible for the current and historical challenges in our world.

♦ **Desire for ownership.** You work hard and smart to create and accumulate assets in amounts sufficient to build an estate for yourself and your family's security and welfare. You are grateful for the things you own, no matter how big or small.

♦ **Desire for a feeling of accomplishment.** Whenever you reach a goal or make a dream come true, you experience a sense of appreciation for the help you received in the process. You feel a sense of self-esteem, fulfillment confidence, happiness, and joy.

♦ **Desire for a feeling of importance.** You want to be recognized for your abilities that lead you to a successful achievement. It may appear to be unimportant to others. However, what you did is important to you. Being recognized is a powerful force to motivate you to bigger and better accomplishments in your life. And ultimately, you'd like to make a difference in the world. Anyone who doesn't receive recognition for positive results may revert to negative actions to receive attention.

♦ **Desire to dream.** You started dreaming of being, doing, and having certain things since you were a child. The human family has progressed so spectacularly, especially during the last 100 or so years, because people dare to dream. They have dreamt of the impossible. Your dreams for the future motivate you to take action today to assure that they become a reality. You may be making sacrifices to enable your children to have funds for a college education. You may dream of a new home, new baby, a new car, a successful marriage, financial freedom, more time with your family, longer vacations, more time to golf, fish, or sail, a carefree retirement or other things.

♦ **Desire for gain.** You want to be rewarded for the work you've done. You want to get ahead so you can live the life you want; being, doing, and having what you truly want in life.

♦ **Desire for safety and security.** You need to accumulate wealth for these two basic wants. Each is a strong motivator because of your desire to be safe and secure in your home and career or business. You look forward to a safe and secure future for yourself and your family. You plan and act specifically to assure loved ones a safe and secure journey through life, as much as possible.

As you grow and develop, you realize more and more that your security is in your ability to produce. As you sense this, and have a track record of achievement, you're more likely to feel safe inside yourself enough to be more adventuresome and risk taking.

Basic Human Frailties

On the other side of the coin, basic human frailties can, if not understood, keep you from realizing your wants and supporting others in doing the same. In order to overcome and cope with frailties, both in yourself and with others, you need to understand that people have them in varying degrees. You need to learn to understand and deal with them in a positive manner. These frailties tend to be more evident in average-thinking people.

Be heartened if you are particularly challenged by any of these weaknesses. We all need to start where we are to get to where we want to be! And where we are just doesn't matter. What really counts is where we're headed! Five of the significant frailties are:

1. **Average-thinking people tend to procrastinate.** Although they may not readily admit it, they have a natural tendency

to put tasks and decisions off. They often need help in making decisions, deciding what is important, and convincing themselves to take action now. Only put off until tomorrow what doesn't need to be done today.

2. **Average-thinking people tend to follow the path of least resistance.** They often make failure-inducing decisions by taking the easy way out. Most people are followers rather than leaders, and are therefore easily influenced by their peers. Unfortunately, their peers are often negative thinking people who are also stuck and aren't moving on either. They may say something like; "I'm not doing it because they're not doing it."

3. **Average-thinking people tend to turn away from challenges.** Most people don't like to face the fact that challenges are a fundamental part of living and being successful. Some of the challenges, like financial difficulties, are common, especially in today's mentality of buy now—pay later. It takes money to live, but to better provide for tomorrow requires delaying gratification today. You may need assistance from your mentor or leader to help you set up a plan to get rid of any debt you may have, so you can move more quickly toward your financial goal.

4. **Average-thinking people lack the willpower to save money.** Average-thinking people shy away from the sacrifices they need to make to save money. A lack of willpower, i.e., self-discipline, is a definite deterrent to saving. If you are experiencing this challenge with yourself, you'll need to be overcome it to make your dreams and goals a reality. Make a commitment to yourself to save enough to first become financially secure and then to accumulate sufficient wealth to achieve financial freedom (which may require supplementing your current income). This will help you make your dreams come true. You will reap rewards by your dedication and perseverance as you continue moving toward your saving objective.

5. **Average-thinking people tend to worry about the future.** They worry about the security of their jobs, future economic conditions, their children's futures, their health, and just about anything else imaginable. Their negative thinking and focus often creates exactly what they're worried about! They

tend to be anxious to find an easy "quick fix" type solution that will relieve them of their worries and anxieties.

An excellent way to help such pessimistic-thinking people is to help them view things differently; in a positive rather than negative manner. This can assist them to reduce or eliminate their concern about the future and replace their negative thinking with a healthy positive expectation. Worry won't improve the outcome, nor increase anyone's life span. It only depletes energy that can be put to much better use!

Staying involved in a continuing education program of positive tapes, books, and seminars and associating with others who are moving on helps to change worry into faith and hope.

You need to understand these basic human wants and frailties, as we all do, so you know what drives yourself and others whom you're helping. This will enable you to take action or respond in a positive and supportive way to both yourself and others. You need to understand that wants and frailties are a normal part of life.

As you continue to develop, you can overcome the frailties and become strong in those areas. This will help you accelerate on your journey of success and avoid the detours that frailties cause you to take. You can then better understand and cope with your own feelings as well as those of others. It'll be easier to have a positive attitude about all the situations you experience and what you observe happening with other people. You can also, with your new level of understanding, lead others to a more substantial and rewarding life for themselves and those around them.

Capabilities

Now to the first word of the C (capabilities) in LUCK. You have capabilities that you developed through your education, environment, observation, and experience. You learn far more from the school of experience than from formal education. Some people have greater capabilities than others do. They specialized and focused their attention on acquiring experience or education or both in a particular area, often to prepare for their job of business.

Such people are usually ordinary people who may be doing extraordinary things because they seriously applied themselves to the task at hand. Perhaps they learned early on that continuous education and fine-tuning is imperative for continued progress toward any worthwhile goal. Are you developing your capabilities, honing your skills at every opportunity to do so? It's up to you to make that choice, which will help you better serve your family and those who could benefit from what you do in your job or business.

Communication

As we discussed before, leaders communicate by their behavior and actions (example), not just by what they say. To communicate effectively, remember that it's 93 percent non-verbal while the words you say account for only 7 percent. Your body language, tone of voice, and what you actually do communicates most of your interest, sincerity, intentions, and feelings. You need to be aware of your body language to be sure it correctly reflects the message you want to send.

As a leader, you need to listen. You need to open your mind and heart to people's ideas, needs, dreams, and goals. The art of listening is vital to effective leadership, and you can't listen and think at the same time. Listening requires patience and practice since our minds can process information much faster than people can talk. So we need to be careful to focus on the person who is sharing. Listen to understand and determine your course of action to best serve your associates, customers, and prospects. This may be in terms of giving guidance, offering mentoring, an opportunity, products, services, or even a referral, as appropriate.

The first President of the U.S., George Washington, wrote, "When another speaks, be attentive yourself, and disturb not the audience. If any hesitate in his words, help him not, nor prompt him without being desired; interrupt him not, nor answer him till his speech is ended." We all need to keep this in mind!

Knowledge

Knowledge is another important ingredient in LUCK. We all have the capacity to obtain more knowledge. Some people consider their learning done once they graduate from high school or college. The truth is that's just the beginning of their learning! People who win are advocates of life-long learning for themselves and others. Our success in maintaining and quenching our thirst for knowledge depends on our attitude, commitment, perseverance, and our willingness to work.

Work could be considered as a combination of Wisdom, Opportunity, Results, and Knowledge. It pulls everything in LUCK together and is an essential ingredient for your success.

I read recently, "Why are some people luckier than others?" The answer is, "Usually it's because they work smarter." And the smarter they work the luckier they get!

As you may recall, another definition of LUCK is when opportunity meets preparation. And since it knocks often, you need to be ready to open the door and allow it to enter your life.

Always remember that your greatest opportunities are found in the *people* you meet and help. This is where real wealth—in fact, all riches in life—can be found.

Chapter Ten

Enthusiasm's Effect On Your Self-Esteem

"The real secret of success is enthusiasm. Yes, more than enthusiasm, I would say excitement. I like to see men get excited. When they get excited, they make a success of their lives."
Walter Chrysler

Your Enthusiasm Makes a Big Difference

It's that certain something that helps you do great things. It pulls you out of the ranks of the mediocre and commonplace and releases your energy. It makes you glow and shine as it lights up your face.

ENTHUSIASM—the emotion that makes you sing and attracts others to sing with you.

ENTHUSIASM—a maker of friends and smiles and a producer of hope and motivation. It shouts to the world, "I've got what it takes and I'm making it happen." It tells all that your career is swell or your business suits you fine, and the goods, services, or opportunity you're offering are the best.

ENTHUSIASM—the inspiration that makes you *wake up and live*. It puts a spring in your step, a song in your heart, a twinkle in your eyes, and it gives you confidence in yourself and others.

ENTHUSIASM—it changes a person with a deadpan personality into one who produces, a pessimistic-thinker to an optimistic one, a person who loafs to a go-getter.

ENTHUSIASM—when you have it, you need to be thankful for it. If you don't have it, you need to develop it.

There is a saying that goes, "Upon the plains of hesitation, bleached the bones of countless millions who, on the threshold of victory, sat down to wait, and waiting they died."

Enthusiasm Is One of Your Greatest Assets

Are you waiting for someone to come along and say, "Boy, have I got a fantastic life for you!" Or are you fired up with enthusiasm about your career or business and your personal life? With enthusiasm, your life and career or business becomes more exciting. The simple mundane tasks become easier to accept. People with enthusiasm like to get going and keep going.

In your private life, you will reap tremendous benefits from your enthusiasm. You'll approach the things you do for fun with a new zest and sparkle. Your friends and family will become much more than just the same old faces you numbly stare at after a challenging day at work. With enthusiasm you can even get those basic household chores done with more ease. You'll enjoy life more because of your excited attitude.

What's the Secret?

As Bertrand Russell once said, "What hunger is in relation to food, zest is in relation to life." How can you unlock the pleasures of this zest, this enthusiasm? There is no magic formula, no mysterious password. It simply starts with you and me and our attitude.

When you're fired up, you're excited to be shown the way. You want immediately to seize the opportunity. The secret to having an enthusiastic attitude is first, you need to be on the lookout for the positive things in your life. And above all, you need to "jump in with both feet," and be adventurous enough and have enough faith to live your life to the fullest. It means embracing life with a childlike sense of wonder and anticipation.

At home, in your business or career, and at play, show genuine enthusiasm for what you do. It's that simple. This approach yields its own opportunities, like attracting other enthusiastic people. But more important is the inner satisfaction you have from being enthusiastic. It lights up your life and the lives of those around you. It's a priceless quality that money simply can't buy.

Fire up your enthusiasm and always carry it with you in your uplifting attitude and manner. It'll spread and positively influence every fiber of your being before you even realize it. Your health will improve, and you will have increased joy, pleasure, satisfaction, and a more significant, fun-filled life.

Someone once said, "With enthusiasm we will be more productive, we will be more efficient, we will be more fulfilled, we will be kinder to each other, and most important, we will have more fun." After all, isn't that basically what life is all about? What if the entire world would live this way? Wouldn't that make an amazing difference?

You may feel you have enthusiasm inside but aren't an extrovert who shows it to others. If this is the case, you might want to start using words that exude enthusiasm. Saying words like wonderful, terrific, excellent, outstanding, and sensational can get you, and those around you, excited. It upgrades and enlivens your communication. It'll make you a positive-thinking people magnet.

Some confuse enthusiasm with impatience. Impatience, however, is being anxious, which is an unhealthy state of mind. While enthusiasm can be helpful in getting a job done effectively, impatience can cause a fanatical, greedy drive to accomplishment. It often leads to errors in judgment and using rather than helping others.

How's Your Self-Esteem?

A key to enthusiasm is to have self-esteem, which as you recall, is the respect you feel for yourself. This healthy self-respect also leads to a sincere respect for others. The ability to keep your life in perspective aids in building self-esteem.

Perspective includes knowing the difference between boredom and elation, being serious and lighthearted, and knowing the difference between truths and falsehoods. We all start out with self-esteem. Then it can be eroded or enhanced as we grow from childhood to adulthood. Developed one way or the other, over a period of time, your self-esteem is a reflection of the beliefs you have about yourself. It's unconsciously formed from past experiences, successes and failures, humiliations and triumphs.

The way you were treated by those most important to you, who you allowed to influence you, could have either built-up or injured your self-esteem. In short, this feeling of respect (or lack of it) you have for yourself turns out to be a kind of life-governing device.

You may never have questioned the validity of your beliefs, so naturally you proceed to act as if they are true. Every day your actions, behavior and feelings are always consistent with and reflective of your self-esteem. When it is intact and secure, you feel peaceful happy, confident, and relaxed. When it is not, you feel unhappy, anxious, and insecure.

Self-esteem fluctuates to some degree for all of us. It's not a constant. People endeavor to hide their lack of it, in many cases, by constantly joking, exhibiting brazen behavior, or trying to look good, be right, and cover (protect) themselves. As people become more developed, associate with people who love and support them, and live with a sense of meaning and purpose, their self-esteem blossoms. They no longer feel the need for the facade they used to hide behind. They learned to better accept themselves, warts and all. They learn all they need to do is to be themselves and continue to do the best they can. Some people will like them and others won't, which is true for everyone. This reality becomes okay with them and they enjoy life.

Psychologists have isolated the one prime cause for success or failure in life. It is the presence of or absence of self-esteem. The key to remaking your self-esteem is to have at least one positive thinking person, perhaps your mentor or leader, who believes in you and supports you. To remake your self-esteem is truly to remake your life, as many who have done it will attest. No person or circumstance can prevent you from improving your self-esteem when you want to make the change strongly enough. The degree to which you improve it will be in exact proportion to the amount of truth about yourself you can take without running away.

You need to reject any self-imposed limitations and do your best to overcome or work around those you can't control, such as some physical or emotional disabilities.

Examples of self-imposed limitations are: a lack of self-confidence, a negative attitude, living as a follower rather than a leader, lack of organization, an attitude of inferiority because you don't have a college education or whatever, the feeling that you don't have or can't earn the respect of your peers or friends, a misconception concerning how your physical appearance may be received by others, or a general lack of self-esteem that you're aware of but not working on.

Don't allow negative thinking people, unaffirming thoughts, or challenging circumstances to steal into your mind like thieves in the night. They'll only rob you of your greatest treasure—intact self-esteem. Close your mind to all restrictions that are under your control. They are only possessions of your own personal false beliefs, which may be yet to be discovered.

Your true self knows no self-imposed limitations. You can break through the falsehoods and regain your precious self-esteem. Many others have done it and so can you. As Helen Keller once said, "When we do the best we can, we never know what miracle is wrought in our life or in the life of another."

Improving Your Self-Esteem

As briefly touched on, your self-esteem can be remade, but like anything else worthwhile, it takes time. If you want to be a more positive, enthusiastic person, you need to strive each day to think and act only in a positive and enthusiastic manner.

You need to make a commitment to improve or dramatically change your self-esteem by picturing and thinking only positive things about yourself. Think about "What kind of a person do I want to be?" If doubts or negative thoughts creep into your mind, let them go. Picture only what you want. Restart your commitment to make the change, if necessary. Be determined and persistent.

If you've taken a golf or tennis lesson, you've probably had the same experience. During the first few days following the lesson, you may not do very well. As you continue, however, to practice, practice, practice in a positive, focused manner, you gradually become better and better at it. At the end of a two or three week period you probably will have mastered the necessary changes to your approach, and your game is likely to be tremendously improved. This same regimen will enable you to upgrade your self-esteem, attitude, skills, and habits that you want to change.

To bolster your self-esteem, as mentioned before, you also need a mentor. You need someone to tell you you're okay as a person and that you're doing great. It's also a good idea to associate with other positive, upbeat people on a regular basis as well to help keep your spirits up and to feel good about yourself.

By acting enthusiastic, you become enthusiastic physically, mentally, and emotionally. And since it is contagious, others around you will catch it. Your self-esteem, the foundation for your enthusiasm and success, will go far to make your journey to your goals and dreams virtually void of restrictions and roadblocks that may be self-imposed. You'll get better at catching yourself putting barriers in your way. Eventually, you'll let go of the habit of thwarting your own success in this way.

Rather than focusing on why you can't do something, you'll focus on how you can instead.

Finally, here's a key question to ask yourself. "Do I feel enough respect for myself to do whatever it takes to give myself the life I want?" Self-esteem is absolutely essential for you to ignite your enthusiasm to succeed and make your dreams come true!

Chapter Eleven

Leadership By Goals and Dreams

*"Unless you give yourself to some great cause,
you haven't even begun to live."*

Successful Leaders Have Big Dreams, Set Big Goals, and Get Big Results

Goals and dreams are essential when you're striving for success.

Without a dream, you have no reason to do anything out of the ordinary. The dream is the single biggest *why* you can have that will literally *make* you do things you wouldn't otherwise do. The bigger your dreams, the more goals you'll set, the more you'll accomplish, and the happier you'll be.

True, leaders are big dreamers, and they can attract others like a magnet. Many people just love to be around a dreamer and their positive energy. Dreaming is contagious, and once you help people start dreaming about something that can improve their life—whether it is a product, service, or an opportunity— your business or career can really grow.

But what is success? Again, "Success is the progressive realization of a worthwhile dream or goal."

It's built on the three cornerstones of goal setting, action planning, and doing whatever's needed to make it a reality. When joined together they form the strong foundation on which all success is created.

Now let's put this definition under the light. "Success is the progressive realization of a worthwhile dream or goal."

Say you have a worthy dream, maybe several. If so, you need to decide which of those dreams you want to experience first. Maybe it's the one you've had the longest, perhaps even since you were a child. Pick the one you're most passionate about achieving.

Goal setting is attaching an achievement date to that dream. When do you want to make it happen? What steps do you need to take to do so? For example, if you want to move to a new level in your organization, what do you need to do to accomplish that? Attach dates to each stepping stone along the way. Ask you leader or mentor to help you or to review your goals and give you guidance.

Next, taking appropriate action results in the progressive realization of those dreams and goals, as long as you keep persisting and resetting the goals, as necessary, until you reach them.

Goal setting and taking action are as inseparable in success as night following day, yet they are equally distinctive. They are heads and tails of the same coin. One says why and what, while the other says how and when. Together they mean success.

Someday Becomes a New Word Called Never!

Having a worthy end-goal or dream without setting intermediate goals and doing the required follow-up activity is mere daydreaming. Someday is a fantasy that becomes a new word called never! To make your goals do-able, it makes sense that you have a way to attain them. A plan of action is needed, but building one loosely described, without goals, is a waste of time and effort.

When you set worthy goals and weld them to a plan of action, *then diligently take that action,* you propel yourself to success.

It's really simple. Why don't most people succeed if it's so simple? Because they fail to follow through. For the same amount of time and energy, in many cases, as they use doing miscellaneous things not leading to their dream, they could have their dream!

Will Rogers, American humorist, once said, "Even if you're on the right track, you'll get run over if you just sit there."

Have you ever started on a trip or vacation without a destination in mind? I bet not. Without a goal, a destination, or a planned route, you'll fail in your quest for whatever you desire. You study a map or call an Automobile Association or travel agency for the shortest or most scenic route. They or you mark the map before you leave for your ultimate destination. You reach it successfully because you had a plan and a goal. If along the way you missed your turn or exit, you backtracked or discovered another workable route to get you to your desired destination. Right?

How about taking this approach with the rest of your life's journeys? When you set a goal and focus on a dream, you'll be amazed at how significant and satisfying the realization of your goal, i.e., your dream, will be. You'll find the trip an adventure in and of itself. It's exhilarating to be in the process and to watch your dream unfold and become your reality.

Just when you are about to reach a short-term goal, if you haven't done so already, you need to immediately set new and higher ones, then continue to work onward and upward. The only way to coast is downhill. There is really no such thing as status quo, because time's moving one. You're losing ground if you're not advancing toward realizing a heartfelt dream. That's why truly happy and successful people know how to work smarter as they progress through life.

The more successful you become in your career or business, the smarter you need to work. The dividends and results you achieve are always relative to the work you do and depending on what you're doing, perhaps more significantly, how many others you inspired to work as well.

On the other hand, non-leaders may reach a short-term goal and stop progressing. They seem to go backward, or downhill, because they are coasting by resting on their laurels. They need to re-ignite their passion about their long-term goal—their dream.

Have you ever noticed how truly successful people seem to continue having success? Conversely, a person who fails often continues to fail. This is the result of either setting a goal, developing a plan of action, and following through to completion, or not even setting a goal in the first place. The choice is yours. If it is to be it's up to you! Once you've identified the dream you're most excited about, set an achievement goal date and develop a plan with short-term goals. Now you're ready for action.

A Guide for Leadership by Goals and Dreams

First, have you established your motivation—your dream? Have you set goals to achieve it?

- What motivates *you?* What do *you* desire? What's *your* dream? You may accept suggestions concerning what you may want. However, you need to identify something *you* strongly and sincerely desire. Don't let circumstances get in your way. You can do anything you believe you can do.
- Write down your goals and the timetable that you're setting.
- As you proceed, periodically evaluate your progress in relationship to the timetable you've set up. Do this with your mentor or leader at mutually agreed upon intervals, perhaps once a month. Have your basic assumptions about what you need to do and how long it takes to do it changed since you first set your goals? If they've changed, you may need to adjust your goals accordingly.

  When certain conditions in your life improve or are eliminated, allowing you to move ahead more quickly, you can reset your goals more ambitiously. If conditions deteriorate, you need to recommit and stay on track more than ever.

  Be determined, persistent, dedicated, and committed, to achieve your goals and to be as flexible as necessary in the process. Adjust your activities accordingly. Your goals need to be attainable, but challenging enough to require you to stretch to achieve them. Incidentally, as you may recall, *realistic* is whatever you believe. So you need to raise your level of belief!
- Don't concern yourself with your current capabilities. When you've got a big enough dream, you can overcome whatever obstacles you encounter along the way.

- Consider the opportunities available. What are the market conditions? What are the economic conditions now and projected? How can you use these conditions to bolster your success? What new products or services will help you achieve your goal? How can you take advantage of e-commerce on the Internet? Does your company have a web page? Always be looking for opportunities to grow your career or business.
- Consider your wants. What income level do you desire? What peer recognition are you striving for? Incorporate these things into your goals. And remember that your goals need to be specific rather than general. You need to have well-defined targets to shoot for.
- What do you really, really want to accomplish? What's the timetable for reaching your goal? What if you only had a year to live? Would that help you give achieving your goal a sense of urgency? Give your goal that urgency now. Time's moving on.
- If you want a new house, what type and price range? Dreambuild regularly by going to open houses on Sunday afternoons. (Which is when real estate agents in the U.S. typically open houses to the public. It may be different if you live elsewhere).
- If you want to start earning and saving more money to be financially free, what amount do you need to accumulate and when do you want it available?
- Your business or career goals may need to include a specific number of presentations per day, week, month, or year, depending on what you're doing.
- Only share your goals with certain others: your supportive family and your leader or mentor. You need to be accountable to them. If you are the only person who knows of your specific goal, and you miss it, no one else will know or care. Will *you* care? You need to look at things as they can be. This will help you to care enough to reach your goals.
- Start fresh when you're setting and striving toward your goals. The past is over and it's time to move on. You need to continue to believe you can do whatever you've decided to

achieve. Do you have a strong work ethic? What changes, if any, in your work ethic will help you reach your goal? Are you going to approach a previously untried prospect? Will you commit to doing more than you've ever done before?

♦ Can you work harder, smarter, or differently to accelerate your realization of your goal? Will your personal situation be used as an excuse not to or a reason to concentrate on your new goal? You need to do *whatever it takes* if you expect to succeed. Do you need guidance from your mentor or leader on this? Ask them for it.

Are you honestly making enough effort to reach your goal? Or are you fooling yourself thinking that just being plugged into a continuing education program and associating with your positive thinking associates will do it? What's the incentive?

1. A sense of accomplishment is undoubtedly one of the greatest dividends you can achieve by diligently following through and reaching your goals and dreams.
2. Productivity increases will be followed by income increases. Money may not be the most important thing in your life; however, it does help compensate for many sacrifices you and your family may make in order for you to reach your goals. It gives you more freedom and choices, when used wisely.
3. Recognition from others for doing something positive is a wonderful dividend. However, true leaders are humble. They recognize that their success is also due to the help they had from their leaders or mentors and perhaps others along the way. They are well aware that it is not a solitary venture, and their humility separates them from the crowd.

Your confidence in all areas of your life can soar when you're persistently pursuing your dream. You'll have that spring in your step and excitement in your eyes.

The Future Belongs to Those Who Prepare for It
Start today, if you haven't already, to practice by being the leader in your life and in your career or business by setting goals,

focusing on your dreams, and encouraging others to do the same. This will help you to be more keenly aware of where you are going. You won't be like many who wonder where they've been and how they got there.

Two important questions you need to ask yourself are: "What business am I in?" The people business, right? (Remember that *all* businesses are people businesses.) And "What is my mission, purpose, and dream?" What drives you to do what you're doing?

Remember that if something is worth doing, it's worth doing poorly until you can do it well. Go for it and if you make mistakes, relax. It's just part of the process. Success comes in the *doing.* With the answers to these questions you can set your priorities and goals.

Is your mission, purpose, and dream clearly defined? Why do you believe you're here on this earth? What can you contribute that's something you enjoy doing? What would you do even if you didn't get paid? What will it take to build your business or career to a certain point?

You need to set goals to begin your journey, but to achieve them—to set your plan into motion—you need to *work.* You need to *plan your work* and then *work your plan,* as covered in chapters four and eight.

While setting your goals, you will be influenced by both your personal and business life. Although it's important that you set goals to satisfy your personal wants and needs, you also need to consider how they will fit into the overall goals of your family. In addition to that, what do they want and how can you support them in getting it?

The direction your goals take is directly related to the impact of your individual desires. What do you *really, really* want to achieve? What have you been pushing to the "back burner"? Will you make the sacrifices you need to? Will you do *whatever it takes,* day by day, to make it happen and be determined not to let circumstances get in your way? Are you going to be bigger than your circumstances?

Another advantage of Leadership by Goals and Dreams is that you have something to focus on and move toward and you can control and measure your performance. This will help you to strongly motivate yourself to continually strive toward your dreams and goals because they are in focus at all times.

Imagine you are being beckoned to come and claim your dream. Think of it as being on layaway, if you will. As you continue to pay the price, i.e., serving more people and reaching your goals, whatever that requires of you, your dream will eventually be paid in full—and become a part of your new reality. You'll own it. Then you get to dream even bigger and do it again. Your life is becoming such an adventure!

Self-Discipline—Another Important Ingredient in Being a Leader

This is a trait you need to have to press on toward your goal. "Desire is the ingredient that changes the hot water of mediocrity to the stem of outstanding success," a wise person once noted. Fortunately, when your desire is strong enough, you're drawn to your dream, rather than being pushed by circumstances. And self-discipline almost automatically follows.

Have you ever heard anyone say the following about someone? "Everything he touches turns to gold. I'll bet that if he fell into a pile of cow manure, he would come out smelling like a rose!"

Why does this seem to be true for some people? As mentioned earlier, people with a goal, a strong enough desire, a positive attitude, and a well-thought out plan and follow through, will succeed in whatever they decide to do. This is true as long as they want it strongly enough and—*they just keep going until they get it.*

Once you've decided you really want to pursue your dream, you need to do *whatever it takes* to reach your goal—things like:

◆ Working extra hard, smart, and longer hours.
◆ Continuing your education by reading positive books, listening to motivational/educational tapes, and going to seminars to improve your knowledge and skills.
◆ Picture in your mind the positive side of an event even though on the surface it could be seen as negative. Look for the good.

- Learn from your negative experiences and challenges. Remember that there is no such thing as failure—it's just a learning experience along the way to your goal.
- Don't be content to be one of the crowd. Instead be a leader and pacesetter.
- Always set a good example for others to follow. Don't expect them to do what you wouldn't do. Again, *walk your talk!*
- Develop your self-esteem and self-confidence, and genuinely care about others and what's happening in their lives.
- Lead people by building their dream or goal and helping them realize it.
- Match and exceed the efforts of others. Take the lead— become a star in your industry!

Look at these things as adventures in taking action. Help those who think mediocrity or failure to turn things around and rise above their challenges. With your caring attitude about people's self-discipline, and perseverance with your positive attitude, it can be done.

Remember that the way we *think* determines our success or failure. Negative thoughts cause negative results, but positive thoughts cause positive results. The foundation of our lives is over thinking!

Those who believe in themselves can reach any goal they realistically set as long as they discipline themselves to do it. And remember that realistic is whatever you *believe* for yourself to be true. Belief can do wonderful things to your life— that you can even change it a lot—when you *really* want to do so. Belief in yourself can lead to whatever success you want as long as you don't believe in other incompatible things.

For example, you may believe you are a go-getter but at the same time you may also believe you need to watch hours of TV or play with your computer to relax after work. Until you shift your thinking to eliminate the contradictory belief, you'll be fighting an uphill battle. What helps here is to identify some leaders in your industry and duplicate their self-discipline and other success inducing attitudes and behaviors. Talk to them and ask for help.

George Bernard Shaw, British play-wright and critic, once said, "People are always blaming their circumstances for what they are. I don't believe in circumstances. The people who get on in this world are the people who get up and look for the circumstances they want, and if they cannot find them, make them."

What Does it Mean to Be "Self-Made"?

How many times have you read or heard of a self-made man or woman? They are all around us and have been for hundreds of years. In fact, in a sense, we're all self-made. The thing of it is, only the successful will admit it! However, self-made needs to be clarified, because no one can become successful without the cooperation of other people to one degree or another! Self-made really refers to your thinking, beliefs, and actions, and your ability to inspire and lead others to act.

Why are Many People "Under the Circumstances"?

Why are some people successful while others are not? Successful people overcome so-called negative circumstances by regarding them as something that helps them grow. As a result, they turn them into positive situations. They use them merely as stepping stones to achieve the success they desire.

Circumstances are neither inherently good nor bad; they just are. And they are important, but only to the extent that we let them be! Your thinking and beliefs determine whether they have either a positive or negative impact on you. The choice is yours. So, why not go for a positive impact?

Many people claim that they would like to improve their circumstances, yet they're unwilling to improve their attitude and develop the skills necessary to do so. Therefore, they remain ineffective and may wonder why they're constantly struggling to reach their goals.

If someone complains about being "under the circumstances," ask them, "What are you doing under there?" Then help them look for the positive and get beyond their self-pity.

Have you ever thought about why different people, in historically the same circumstances and environment, succeed while others fail? *Desire, belief, attitude, planning, and action make the difference.* As Henry Ford once said, "If you think you can or if you think you can't, you're right." So, think you can and that others can too!

The dictionary defines circumstance as—"a condition, fact, or event accompanying or determining an occurrence of another fact or event; an essential condition of a fact or event."

It might appear, therefore, that our circumstances control us. Why? Simply because most people act or react to them as promptly and completely as they would to a superior's directive. Have you ever noticed that?

Can You Change Your Circumstances?

Is it possible to change the circumstances in your life so you can be more positive and productive?

Perhaps not. If that's the case, you're faced with a challenge. Aren't you?   What do leaders who win do? They discipline themselves to conquer their obstacles. They become stronger and more empathetic through overcoming adversity and are better able to lead others to help them achieve their goals. If they're under the circumstances, by golly, they don't stay there long!

Someone once commented that, "There are times in everyone's life when something constructive is born out of adversity…when things seem so bad that you've got to grab your fate by the shoulders and shake it."

You will encounter many circumstances in your life; some are within your direct control, while others are beyond it. How well you handle these circumstances will largely dictate your progress in achieving your goals and realizing your dreams. Your inclination and readiness to handle these situations promptly and effectively will be apparent from your results.

There are some circumstances that are expected, while others will seem to appear out of nowhere. A positive attitude, confidence, and self-esteem will allow you to more easily confront those unexpected circumstances and overcome any obstacles that may appear. But another piece of good news is that dealing with and overcoming challenging situations can help you strengthen your optimism, build your confidence, and develop your self-esteem. As you meet and courageously overcome circumstances, you can clear the path to your dreams and goals and acquire the results you are striving for.

People who win are usually excellent leaders who actually put forth more effort, perform better, and accomplish more with adversity as their companion. They rise above their circumstances, refusing to use them as an excuse not to achieve their goal. They refuse to be a victim of their circumstances.

There's another benefit of disciplining yourself to push ahead and conquer the obstacles that threaten to thwart your progress. As you go, you become more interested in what you're doing, which in turn endears you even more to your goal! Remember— *where there's no investment there's no value.*

As you do whatever's needed to hurdle your challenges, you're investing yourself in the goal-achieving process, giving it more value. It's easier to keep going because you've already put your blood, sweat, and tears into it. And by goodness, you're *not* going to quit now! So you persevere until you get it done.

A self-motivated person determines what they truly want, sets goals, develops a plan of action, and puts the plan into motion. This not only benefits themselves, but also their family, business or career associates and others who are positively affected by what they're doing. Everyone wins.

There are nine words that say it all—*if it is to be, it's up to me!*

Chapter Twelve

The Art Of Leading Others For Positive Accomplishment

"Time and money spent in helping men to do more for themselves is far better than mere giving."
Henry Ford

Are You a Leader?

Do you recall from earlier in this book whether management and leadership are the same? While there are many traits and talents needed by both, there are just as many that separate them. The main difference is, as you may remember, we manage activities but lead people!

A leader is defined as one who leads; a guide; a conductor; a chief commander. A leader sets the example for others to follow and encourages them to do things they wouldn't do without the leader's influence.

Much of this chapter is based on my career of leading an insurance agency. The concepts and ideals are valuable regardless of the business or profession you're in. They are also useful in dealing with the personal aspects of your everyday life.

Understanding the art of leadership is fundamental to becoming an effective leader.

The single most important thing in building a strong, dynamic organization, is the leader's attitude. And, of course, it needs to be positive! This, combined with an attitude of compassion, understanding, and firmness toward their followers, makes a winning combination. To do this, you need to strongly believe in what you're doing and not let anyone buy into any pity parties. Others may commiserate with these people but it's your job to lead them out of their quagmire and on to success.

Whatever you do personally and professionally, you need to have leadership abilities in specific areas of your life. A homemaker and mother manages her activities (although we may marvel at how) between caring for a home, children, and spouse. In many cases, she also makes time for social and other activities, which may include helping her husband with a business.

A business owner often needs to wear many hats as a leader of various and diverse aspects of their business—buying, selling, sharing, presenting, advertising, counseling, teaching, motivating, building relationships, and miscellaneous and other human relations activities. Bus drivers need to manage their route to maintain a schedule. High school students need to manage to coordinate their study, sports, social, and household commitments.

Ten Keys to Effective Leadership

As a leader, you'll want to maximize the results of your efforts. Here are ten principles that are decisive to a leader's performance and effectiveness:

- ♦ Think extensively of yourself as a leader. Be enthusiastic, and above all, be optimistic. Always look for the good in people and situations. Lead others to do the same.
- ♦ Develop bifocal vision. Focus on two of the most important ingredients in your career or business—people and productivity.
- ♦ Be effective and set priorities. As you may recall, there is a big difference between being effective and being efficient. Efficient people are maintainers. Efficiency is doing things right, whether they're the most important things to do or not. Effectiveness is doing the right things right; putting your energy where it counts the most.

- ◆ Build on two success factors: respect for your organization and, if there are leaders above you, confidence in their leadership.

- ◆ Teach your new associates the system of success in your industry, the key things they need to know and do. It's important for you to know and help them focus on their goals and dreams so they have a reason to excel. But equally, if not more significant, is how you teach them. They need to be taught and led by your superb example. Don't assume they know anything about the business or organization you're in. Start from the beginning with the basics of a proven system that people can understand and duplicate to progressively realize their goals and dreams.

- ◆ Lead by positive expectation. As a role model, give your associates something to live up to.

- ◆ Be an edifier. Admire and respect your leaders, if you have some, for the contribution they've made to the organization. It will then be more likely that your associates will admire and respect you. Compliment both your leaders and your associates on their abilities to give self-confidence. It's a sad fact that 97 percent of the people sell themselves short. Build your associates' self-esteem. Point out their positive attributes and what they're doing well. Encourage them, and assure them that they can do it.

- ◆ Lead by commitment. You need to encourage your new associates to have a high level of commitment. If you're not committed, it's likely they won't be either. So strengthen your commitment if you need to. Establish an excellent relationship with them. Build a friendship and a "success-ship" with them. Help them set goals and reach them. Dreambuild often.

  Help others to teach them how to focus on what they really want by test driving their dream car together, cutting out pictures of what they want and posting them where they can see them, watching an inspiring video, or just imagining how life could be. When you help enough other people get what they want, you'll automatically get what you want. Teach them to stretch and grow toward their potential, by your example of doing the same.

♦ Make every occasion a great one. Recognize your associates' first success as they learn new skills and reach new levels. Again, sincerely compliment them at every opportunity to show you care about their success. Be a goodfinder.

♦ Believe and use the law of cause and effect. "As ye sow, so shall ye reap." Every effect (result) has a cause. Be sure you, as a leader, as well as the people you're leading, understand this law. Following your leadership and guidance could be a major cause of their future successes, depending on how well you lead them. You have the responsibility to show them the direction they need to head to achieve their goals and dreams.

Remember this: where you've been or where you are is not important. *It's where you're headed that really matters.* In your training you need to demonstrate these qualities, but keep it simple. Be consistent, predictable and dependable, and use the power of repetition. If they don't get it at first, repeat your teaching until they do.

The System is the Key

In the above list, I mentioned a system. This refers to following a proven pattern developed by the people in your industry of doing the things that lead to success. This means understanding and following a schedule, method, and design taught by the training and continuing education program. Methodical techniques and general procedures need to be followed to maximize everyone's potential for success. If you're new and unsure of them, get the specifics from your leader or mentor.

Every associate needs to be taught the basics of their business or profession. Some leaders make the mistake of assuming everyone understands these basics. Even if they do, repetition is beneficial so they pick up their leader's or mentor's attitudes on the principles that are important for them to achieve their dreams and goals. They also need to know the basics so well that they can teach others. This removes that one-to-one responsibility from you and gives it to them. This helps you duplicate what you do through others, and grow your business or profession.

If someone attempts to lead by personality alone, they will never be an effective leader. You need to have established procedures in place, which will allow your people to grow and become the best they can be. As *leaders,* we bring out the best in others by giving the best of ourselves.

Personal Development Is Essential for Success

Personal development, the development of yourself, is an essential responsibility for those who want to lead. And for those who want to grow in their leadership skills so they can expand their business or profession, personal development is a key ingredient.

A continuing education program in your business or profession, as well as in leadership philosophies and principles, is key. It will keep you growing and setting the example for your associates to follow. This includes books, tapes, training seminars, conventions, and other activities. Listen to motivational and educational tapes daily, and read 15-30 minutes a day from a positive book. Take advantage of all the continuing education tools and opportunities available to you.

Organizational and corporate magazines and newsletters, both print and online, are an excellent way to keep up to date on the developments in your industry. You also need to participate in your organization. Attend as many organizational meetings and seminars as you can and encourage your associates to do the same. Whenever appropriate, offer to help with set up and the other jobs related to running a meeting or seminar. Go the extra mile. Keep absorbing new and exciting information and associate with people who are also moving on. This will help keep you motivated and on track as well.

Of course, no one else can do your personal development for you! Your attendance and involvement at industry-related seminars will enable you to hone your skills, absorb new ideas, and keep up your enthusiasm. They will also help you develop an important byproduct—*self-confidence.* They will reinforce what you've learned so far, as well as give you recognition, in many cases, of your most recent level of achievement.

It is also important that the people you're leading attend the seminars and see you in action there. Set an example for them to follow—people do what you do much more than what you say. Back up your words with *action*. Show them that you are taking advantage of industry-related continuing education tools and opportunities and they're likely to do the same.

How Are You at Decision Making?

Decision making, or the lack of it, is one of the most serious issues in business and life today. People frequently hesitate or won't make a decision they will be held responsible for. They're often afraid they'll make a mistake or perhaps even be rejected by their peers who perhaps aren't moving on. The leader's decision making process gives him an opportunity to be a champion. He'll lead effectively or stay stuck and languish in mediocrity, depending on his strengths and weaknesses.

When a decision needs to be made, gather the facts and consider the alternatives. While it is important to make a decision, it is also imperative to know exactly what and who the decision will effect. What is the question or circumstance the decision is based on? Have both sides been given the chance to air their views? Is the decision an appropriate response to the question or circumstance? Does it provide a win-win solution? In making effective decisions be open-minded, consider options, and counsel with someone more knowledgeable and experienced, so you can profit by their recommendations.

In your desire to make a decision to launch something new or to solve a pressing challenge, first you need to stop worrying about it. That just saps your energy. Do your best to make a quality decision, then make it right. You might think of it as the ready-fire-aim approach. Just jump in there and give it your all.

Continued worry will not change any situation. It usually keeps you spinning your wheels in a paralysis of analysis. Once you make a decision and the wheels of progress are rolling, the results will be rather automatic. From there, you give it your best shot—whatever the results turn out to be. You take responsibility, adjust things as necessary, and keep on going.

While going through the decision making process, select the most significant task. Focus on it, and you'll be amazed at how well and quickly you can realize your goal. When it is completed, you can go on to other priorities with a clear and open mind. You will be more effective because you'll have made the decision and you're then free to implement it and move on to the next thing of importance.

More Key Skills for Effective Leadership

♦ You need to know what to do and how to do it, so you can lead by example. If you expect your people to make presentations, you need to be proficient in this area so they can watch and duplicate you. The same is true no matter whom you are leading or what you'd like them to do.

♦ You need to have people skills—*the ability to work effectively with others.* As mentioned before, an excellent leader's success is based 95 percent on people skills with as little as 5 percent on product or service knowledge. For example, be considerate of others. And be able to communicate clearly so you are understood and you understand what others are relaying back to you. If others don't do what you're suggesting or needing, you haven't totally communicated with them. Your results tell you how effective you are.

♦ Again, problem solving skills and decision making skills are also essential. Be solution oriented.

♦ You need to be humble and teachable at all times. We all need others to do their part, in order for us to be successful. To think otherwise is foolish. Unhealthy pride, i.e., egotism or arrogance, never serves anyone.

♦ Continuous self-development programs are essential to your growth. The finest leaders are always learning and growing. If people stop learning and growing they start dying. Stay fresh. Keep learning and growing.

A leader can easily master knowledge by study, learning, and doing. Skills and humbleness are learned most effectively and quickly by experience. Experience, sometimes referred to as "the school of hard knocks," is invaluable as you progress through life. You do something new and often get immediate feedback, either through our own gut feeling or the response of others.

Taking action can give you confidence, which has no substitute when you are leading people. This, of course, is provided you don't take yourself too seriously and mentally beat yourself up, as you're going through the learning process. As you develop competence in these basic skills, you can teach and instill confidence in the people you're leading. You've done and are doing what you're teaching them to do. As long as you stay humble in the process, you can shine as a leader.

Think and Plan

To be an effective leader, you need to think and plan. Set aside time for this every day. Helpful ideas will usually come to you after some careful, committed thought and research on your part. When that happens, let go of your conscious thoughts and allow your subconscious mind to take over.

Sleep on an idea or challenge, and you'll be amazed at how it gels the next day.

Thomas A. Edison, renowned inventor, would consciously think about and research ideas, then he would take a short nap. (This, of course, relaxed his conscious mind.) Upon awakening, his subconscious mind would take over, and wonderful new ideas would appear.

Norman Cousins once said, "We in America have everything we need except the most important thing of all—(the habit of taking) time to think and the habit of thought, which is the basic energy in human history. Civilization is put together not by machines but by thought."

Your best insights occur when you are not consciously thinking about the situation in question. The solution to a challenge or a useful new idea will hit you seemingly like a bolt out of the blue.

These ideas don't come out of nowhere. A wealth of conscious thought, research, and concern goes on before hand. The point is, however, after you do this research and thinking, and you're still not coming up with what you need, it's time to let it go for the time being, i.e., stop thinking about it, and go do something else. The ideas or solutions will appear later with no further conscious thought.

A professor at Princeton University put it this way; "Chance favors a prepared mind."

It's best not to worry about things you can't control. It's key though to change your attitude to one of acceptance. If you believe you must worry, set aside a time just to worry! In my busy schedule I set aside every Tuesday afternoon from 2 p.m. to 3 p.m. as my worrying period. I worry about this or that but when 3 p.m. came and the alarm went off, I didn't worry until the next week at the same time!

For more ideas on handling worry see Dale Carnegie's classic book, *How To Stop Worrying And Start Living.* But remember that worry won't extend your life one second, and it really won't change an outcome. You'll just use a lot of energy getting yourself all worked up that you could better use to pursue your dream or to do something else of value.

Another excellent idea is to take time from your busy schedule to think. Make an appointment with yourself for one or two hours each week. When the appointed time comes, put all else aside. After informing others, who might interrupt, that you aren't available, close the door and turn off the phone. Sit back, relax and focus on your dreams and goals. Picture your dreams coming true.

Amazing, productive, and profitable ideas will flow from your subconscious mind. The great side effects of this quiet thinking period are that you will feel wonderful, excited, positive, and worthwhile. This experience may sound trite, but it works.

Leadership—More Food for Thought

Here are five facts about leadership that deserve to be mentioned. These are neither positive nor negative; they just are:

1. Set priorities and do those things that need to be done to reach your goals and dreams or at least to continue your

progression toward them. Follow your plan. Make one if you haven't already done so.

2. Knowing what to do is certainly important but follow-up action is also essential. Behavior is visible, knowledge is not. For example, knowing how to read but not reading is worse than not knowing how to read.

3. Learn to listen; nothing is learned while talking. Listen not only to what people say, but also listen beyond their words to what they don't say. This is often the real message. Listen with empathy. Maybe all they need right now is for you to quietly listen. They may need to know someone cares.

4. See yourself as you really are. You may not always like what you see but what you see probably represents at least some truth about who you are. Be honest with yourself. Write down all the positive qualities you can about yourself. Then list any traits you have that you'd like to change. To change, you need to know what you're changing from.

5. Leadership is where you don't get paid for the work you do but for the results you achieve and inspire others in your organization to achieve.

More On Listening

As you recall, listening is an important part of effective communication. Listening and truly hearing and understanding what others are saying are not the same. We can listen without understanding, but we can't understand without truly listening and perhaps, as a result, asking relevant questions to get clarification.

Empathic listening is paying close attention to what is being said. So always listen with an open, uncluttered mind. Don't be thinking of what you'll say to in response until they have stopped talking. Quiet your mind and focus on the person talking and really hear and understand what they are saying. If you allow yourself to think of other things while pretending to listen, the talker usually picks up the feeling that you don't really care. The only way for them to feel understood is for you to truly listen. Good conversation is a dialogue, not a duel of monologues.

And always remember this—*people don't care how much you know until they know how much you care!* Leadership is built more on this idea than practically anything else. People are more likely to follow those who truly *listen* to them. Listening shows you care. Few people do it well and you'll stand out more as a leader when you truly listen!

Observe and Counsel

An effective leader is also a good observer and counselor. One idea that works wonders is to periodically sit down with people you are leading. Review precisely what has happened and what their goals are for tomorrow, next week, next month, and next year. In many cases, a monthly review is effective to help keep people on track and moving in the direction they need to go to reach their goals.

Be sure to cover these items when you get together:

1. They need to know what they need to do to be successful each day, week, month, and year.
2. They need to know what they are doing well which is usually reflected in their results. (Note: I say "usually," because your people could be making excellent presentations and yet are still going through a string of noes. They'd just need to keep on going, that's all.)
3. They need to know where they need to improve their knowledge and skills.
4. They need to know what else, if anything, they can do to produce better results. For example, it's a generally known fact that people tend to trust men more who are clean-shaven. Your associate may need to shave his beard off. Or he may need to use deodorant or shower daily! There are books and tapes that cover these topics and others regarding personal hygiene . You could steer your associate toward purchasing the book or tape.

How Are Your Relationship Building Skills?

Skills in relationship building are central to your growth as a leader. The relationships you build with your people are more consequential than any talent you may have. You could have all the talent in the world, but if you don't build excellent relationships, you have no one to share it with and assist. Talent is the capacity for top-notch performance in a specific area.

With a caring, growth-supporting, and cooperative relationship of mutual respect with others, along with a positive attitude, your people's performance can improve dramatically—whether or not they're particularly talented to start with. They can make up for it with courage, determination, a teachable attitude, and extra effort. With all those qualities, they just may outshine your most talented people who aren't as motivated! *Talent or other qualities, when multiplied by your relationships, leads to increased productivity.*

Always remember that while nobody can do everything, everyone can do something. Your function as a leader is to help people do what they do best—to bring out the best in people. Surround yourself with self-motivated people who, step by step, are making progress toward success. Create a positive environment so that your people will find the road of success as smooth and well paved as possible. Be there to encourage them over the "bumps" too!

Participative Leaders Get the Best Results

There are at least two distinct styles of leadership—autocratic and participative.

♦ *Autocratic leaders* have a dictatorial attitude. They have and are the power. They make all decisions by themselves (and for themselves, even if they don't realize it). Such leaders operate through manipulation and intimidation, instilling fear in their people. It's an archaic way of thinking that destroys rather than creates any potential for positive relationships. Such leaders want yes people who won't disagree with their ideas to surround them. This style builds resentment and hostility and actually motivates people to move away from their leadership—to escape their tyranny, if they have the courage to do so.

♦ *Participative leaders* believe in the potential of their people. They see people for what they can become, rather than how they are right now. They express their feelings which come from their hearts, and have a personal caring philosophy, and a positive expectancy of their people. They offer honest compliments, encouragement, and support. They help their associates identify and get what they want.

Leaders Need to Be Flexible

Some personalities need more participation and guidance from their leader, while others are perhaps more confident self-starters who can do more on their own. Effective leaders are flexible and adapt to the needs of their people.

Remember, the primary objective of a leader is to *maximize the productivity of their people*—so they can all reach or exceed their individual goals. This then enables the leader to reach or exceed their own goals.

A leader's responsibility is not to have command over people. It is responsibility for contributing to the success of an organization and its people. Function, not power, is the business of a leader.

Like the old saying goes, "Give a man a fish and he'll eat for a day. Teach a man to fish and he'll eat for a lifetime."

The successful leader trains and handles each individual differently, according to that person's needs. People have different personal histories, values, ideals, personalities, beliefs, goals, and dreams. And it's these differences that help to make leadership an exciting and challenging adventure. (No two people are the same!) Your ability to recognize and respect these differences and lead others on their journey of a progressive realization of their worthwhile goals and dreams can result in superb leadership and tremendous success all the way around.

Chapter Thirteen

Essentials For High Performance Leadership

"Get a good idea and stay with it. Dog it and work at it until it's
done, and done right."
Walt Disney

Do You Have These High Performance Leadership Qualities?
When I talk about leaders here, I'm referring to excellent leaders who serve as role models for all of us. Such leaders possess vision and have a mission to guide them and their organization. They know the difference between efficiency and effectiveness. They strive each day to be as effective as possible by doing goal-achieving tasks rather than just tension relieving, maintenance related tasks that can by done by others or left undone. They know that to attract other fine leaders or potential leaders they need to be exemplary leaders themselves.

Leaders point the way for others to follow, not just out of obedience but from understanding. Leaders listen with empathy because they care about their people, and they, to one degree or another, have been in similar situations. They are proactive rather than reactive, which is how average thinking people tend to act. They definitely make things happen, and often in a big way.

Leaders exude enthusiasm, a positive attitude, a strong commitment, and sincere dedication. They earn their people's trust because of their unshakable integrity and impeccable honesty. They are gracious, humble, appreciative, and always in a learning and growing mode. Intact self-esteem, healthy self-confidence, and consistent self-discipline are also marks of high performance leadership.

Leaders backup their words with appropriate action. As Edgar Guest, American writer and poet, once said:

Sermons We See

"I'd rather see a sermon than hear one any day;
I'd rather one should walk with me than merely tell the way.
The eye's a better pupil and more willing than the ear,
Fine counsel is confusing, but example's always clear;
And the best of all the preachers are the men who
live their creeds,
For to see the good in action is what everybody needs.

I can soon learn how to do it if you'll let me see it done;
I can watch your hand in action, but your tongue
too fast may run.
And the lecture you deliver may be very wise and true,
But I'd rather get my lesson by observing what you do;
For I might misunderstand you and the high advice you give,
But there's no misunderstanding how you act
and how you live.

When I see a deed of kindness, I am eager to be kind.
When a weaker brother stumbles and a strong man stays behind
Just to see if he can help him, then the wish grows strong in me
To become as big and thoughtful as I know that friend to be.
And all travelers can witness that the best of guides today
Is not the one who tells them, but the one
who shows the way.

One man teaches many, men believe what they behold;
One deed of kindness noticed is worth forty that are told.
Who stands with men of honor learns to hold his honor dear,
For right living speaks a language which to every one is clear.

Though an able speaker charms me with his eloquence, I say,
I'd rather see a sermon than to hear one any day."

The Finest Leaders Create a People-Oriented Environment

Leaders have the ability to generate an environment in which others feel at ease, free to be themselves, and appreciated. Effective leadership requires heartfelt compassion, sensitivity, and sound judgment concerning people and how to best treat them.

Leaders get most of their work done through people, and only do themselves what they are best at and cannot delegate to others. They believe in and encourage teamwork up and down the line. They strengthen human relations by allowing and encouraging their associates to be an integral part of planning for what they'll be doing. They delegate responsibilities according to their people's strengths and preferences as much as possible—knowing where they'll shine the most, i.e., be the most productive. They realize everyone has a valuable role—*no one* has an unimportant part to play on the team.

Top-Notch Leaders Inspire Rather Than Just Require

Rather than telling people what to do, leaders have the *ability to inspire others* to follow their lead to reach a goal or a dream. They develop charisma, which is the balancing of opposite qualities into a personality that almost anyone can identify with. These qualities include genuinely upbeat and positive thinking; extremely kind, compassionate, and warm; gentle yet strong; delightful to be around; friendly yet not aggressive; unfailingly encouraging and hope-inducing; and self-assured yet amazingly humble. They are what people relate to the most.

Boy, you might be saying, "That's a *lot* to live up to!" People don't become this way overnight. Fortunately, though, these qualities can be learned and acquired through your environment, experience, and following the lead of others. What qualities might you need more of to create the right balance yourself? Whatever they may be, start practicing them today! Most people have the talent, capacity, and education to perform far better than they ever choose to do. This includes developing charisma—that special something that sets you apart from the crowd.

Will needs to accompany skill. Will is a compelling desire combined with determination. Do you desire success "badly enough" to be more and better than you've ever been and to do more than you've ever done? Edison once said, "If we would do all we were capable of doing, we would astound ourselves."

Everyone needs inspiration at various times in their lives. Some more than others! It's the leader's responsibility to provide it by taking a sincere interest in their people and setting a fine example for others to follow.

Leaders need to find and develop will in people. This can only be done by discovering their "hot buttons"—their dreams—and cultivating them. This ignites their will. It's a fun challenge because no two people think alike or are motivated by the same desires and beliefs. This helps make leadership such an adventure and a growing experience!

What's the Difference Between a Boss and a Leader?

The following comparison between a boss and a leader was presented during a seminar on leadership. (Author unknown, from Kinder Brothers, Patterns of Professional Management):

Be A Leader

"The boss drives his men; the Leader coaches them.
The boss depends on authority, the Leader on goodwill.
The boss inspires fear; the Leader inspires enthusiasm.
The boss says 'I'; the Leader says 'We.'

The boss says; 'Get here on time';
The Leader gets there ahead of time.
The boss fixes blame for the breakdown;
The Leader fixes the breakdown.

The boss knows how it is done; the Leader shows how.
The boss says, 'Go'; the Leader says, 'Let's go.'

The boss uses people; the Leader develops them.
The boss sees today; the Leader also looks at tomorrow.

The boss commands; the Leader asks.
The boss never has enough time;
The Leader takes time for things that count.
The boss is concerned with things;
The Leader is concerned with people.

The boss lets his people know where he stands;
The Leader lets his people know where they stand.
The boss works hard to produce;

The Leader works hard to help his people produce.
The boss takes the credit; the Leader gives it away."

Qualities of a High Performance Leader

High performance leaders have specific qualities, some of which we touched on before, that are part of their deep-rooted philosophies and principles. Here are 25:

- ♦ They are possibility thinkers—solution-oriented rather than problem-oriented.
- ♦ They are loyal toward their organization, industry, and associates.
- ♦ They love and accept themselves unconditionally and do the same for others.
- ♦ They have conviction of their beliefs and values, and they live by them.
- ♦ They are decisive. They work with their team to gather the facts, evaluate them, weigh the recommendations, make a decision, and then live by it.
- ♦ They strive to treat all their associates fairly. "Do unto others as you would have others do unto you." If they fail at this, they quickly make amends and apologize for their unskillful behavior to the wounded party.
- ♦ They are basically even-tempered and predictable in all their relationships. They have a good sense of where they stand and what they stand for.
- ♦ They share the limelight. They know they didn't get where they are alone and they readily admit it. They give credit to and appreciate any assistance, big or small, that they received.
- ♦ They lead by example, constantly fine-tuning their own skills. "Do as I do, not just as I say!"
- ♦ They have impeccable morality. They earn respect by their personal behavior.

◆ They show heartfelt enthusiasm and an unrelenting positive attitude in all they do. Their enthusiasm is contagious, and their associates almost inevitably catch it.

◆ They know the importance of building the self-esteem of their people because of the direct relationship between self-esteem and peak performance.

    They help to keep their people motivated and growing though plugging them into positive books, tapes, and seminars.

◆ They accept responsibility for all of their actions. If a decision was incorrect, they remember it was their decision, own up to it, and take remedial action.

◆ They communicate their goals and dreams to their leader or mentor.

◆ They delegate authority to others—helping them feel they are a valuable part of their team—which causes the team members to feel good about themselves and their roles.

◆ They keep communications open and encourage honest feedback. They root out rumors and do their best to get to the bottom of them before they spread and create disharmony, fear, and potential chaos. They don't gossip—they talk about ideas and feelings, rather than people.

◆ They are excellent, focused listeners. They realize they learn nothing while they're talking. So they strive to listen more than talk.

◆ They dare to dream and dreambuild constantly, always going for bigger dreams to keep themselves motivated. They also dreambuild regularly with their associates to keep them going and teach them to do the same, for themselves and down the line.

◆ They don't take themselves too seriously, have a great sense of humor, and make things fun.

◆ They are service oriented in all they do in their career or business.

◆ They have the faith and inner strength to face obstacles, setbacks, and failures without being diverted from their mission.

◆ They are confident about their ability to help others fulfill their mission.

- They love their work. They know that they'll do their best by sticking to tasks they enjoy and are good at. They delegate the other things that other people are good at and enjoy. They know everyone benefits from this approach.
- They pursue their mission or vision with passion, conviction, commitment, and persistence—until it becomes a reality.
- They develop a patient, yet forward moving attitude. They keep on going, doing what they need to do. Yet they know challenges arise and a delay is not a denial. They learn not to try to force things to happen—there's a time and place for everything.

What Is Your Mission?

Winston Churchill, former Prime Minister of England once said, "The price of greatness is responsibility."

Leaders have a responsibility to establish and live by their mission. A mission is a statement of where you want to go and how you want to get there. It is not a goal but an ideal that reflects the values and principles that you are building in your business or career. Sit down with your leader or mentor and business partner(s) if you have any (perhaps your spouse?) and put together a mission statement you can both (or all) agree on. From then on, you need to base your actions on values and principles that are part and parcel of your mission.

A sample mission statement might be—"Our mission is to help people grow and become all they were meant to be as they strive for their goals and dreams. We will promote the established system of success for our industry including our comprehensive continuing education program as the simplest and most effective way our associates can achieve their dreams and goals. We will help them build their businesses or careers with matched effort on our part, and compliment, teach, and encourage them every step of the way."

Do You Have the Attitude of a Servant-Leader?

A servant-leader does whatever is required to meet the needs of their customers and clients and support their staff or associates. Although it may not appear a servant-leader is in a power position—some may even believe it's a slave posture—it makes for the best leaders. Slaves, however, do whatever their master wants and are not in a decision-making role, whereas a servant-leader is. It's the responsibility of such a leader to determine what the needs are of the people they serve, which may differ from what these people think they want.

To clarify what a servant-leader does, here's an example: You may have an inexperienced employee or associate who requests you to make a telephone call to a customer or prospect because they're afraid to make the call. As a servant-leader, you take charge. You support your employee or associate in facing and overcoming their fear and help them develop and fine-tune their skills and knowledge base so they can make the call themselves.

The most ideal result is not necessarily that they have a yes from the customer or prospect, although it would be a plus, for sure. The main goal here, though, is to teach and encourage this person to have more confidence in themselves and learn to, at least in part, duplicate what you do. Otherwise you forever remain their slave! You want them to not only learn what to do and apply themselves to the task, but to be capable of teaching others, along the line. This admittedly tosses out any old thinking that you don't want this person to replace you. As you're moving on in your company or organization, you're learning and growing, and ideally fostering the same degree of growth in those who look, hopefully with respect, to you as their leader.

You may be saying, "I'm not a leader; I don't oversee or supervise anyone." That could well be true, in a formal sense. However, servant-leadership, or any other kind of leadership, is taken—*not given!*

As you prove to be a leading edge person who takes charge of your responsibilities and has a service-oriented attitude, you become a leader. You care about others and apply yourself as a valuable member of the team.

Real servant-leaders are at a premium; so fear not, you'll be noticed! Having a servant-leader attitude and acting like one is usually, if not always, at the center of being a happy professional or business leader. It's the opposite of a begrudging attitude, which many people have about the work they do. And, as you've undoubtedly noticed, those with such an attitude are definitely *not* happy, no matter what they happen to be doing. It's an inside job. (You become a leader within and of yourself first.) So actually, you are a leader, if not officially, in so much as your attitude is always an example to others. It's likely you have a much bigger influence on those around you than you may now think.

You may be asking, "How can I be a servant-leader with my customers and prospects? Am I not supposed to give them what they want?" In some cases, what your customer or prospects want is what they need. But frankly, in many other cases, they only *think* they know what they want. It's your job to discover what they really need and determine how you can best serve them.

Oftentimes the customer or prospect has an uneducated, preconceived notion of what you're sharing with them. If this weren't the case, they wouldn't need you to inform them would they?

Even if you are relatively new and inexperienced in your industry, chances are you know more than your prospect or customer. If you don't know an answer to one or more of their questions, it's certainly legitimate to say so and get back to them with the answer as soon as you can.

It does take effort and courage to educate these people, but for these who choose not to go this "extra mile" such a customer or prospect is generally not won.

To sum it up, people with a servant-leader attitude and approach are the ones who aren't only generally happier, but who also create win-win all around scenarios, wherever they may be.

Fine Leaders Have a Positive Impact on Society

Leaders have the ability and the responsibility to have a positive impact on our society. Your character and integrity as a leader will have an up-lifting effect on the people you lead.

Your strongly held values and principles which are the very evident foundation for the actions you take, could well be embraced by a large number of people, both within and outside your immediate circles of influence. Your guidance through your excellent example, could be the catalyst to cause your organization to progress to higher standards.

Your high moral values will contribute to our society in the coming trend of returning to "old fashioned" traditional morality. Your unwavering principles can help unite your people to work together to pursue the goals and dreams that raise their quality of life, and at the same time fulfill the mission you have set forth for your organization.

Leaders are made, not born. People don't usually set out to be a leader, but because of their willingness to express themselves openly and freely, they evolve from followship to leadership. They grow from the silent majority to the contributing minority. They are not out to prove anything; rather, they want to communicate and share their creative ideas, thereby influencing others in the natural process.

High performance leadership is easier for those who are positive, confident, and willing to work hard and smart to help others. Those without these qualities at the outset need to develop them. The opportunities for leadership are everywhere for those who are willing to accept these responsibilities and challenges.

Leaders focus on people's strengths rather than dwell on their weaknesses. They build the confidence of their associates and others in their life by recognizing their beautiful attributes and assisting them to work on their success-stealing qualities. Remember, no matter how developed we are, we all have weaknesses—patience is needed with others, and ourselves, too!

Leaders love and respect other people. They appreciate what their people *can* do and don't laugh at or be otherwise negative about the skills they haven't mastered yet. Confidence can be instilled and self-esteem built by helping them build positive expectations and recognizing them for what they do well. Leaders then work to help them develop in other skill areas where they need it, as much as possible.

Leaders Gather Their Courage and Take Risks

Ralph Waldo Emerson once said, "Whatever course you decide upon, there is always someone to tell you that you are wrong. There are always difficulties arising that tempt you to believe that your critics are right. To map out a course of action and follow it to the end requires ... courage."

Leaders need to go ahead and take risks. If they don't, not only won't they succeed in their venture, but they'll also never know if they even could have succeeded had they "taken the plunge." Without courage, nothing much outside of the ordinary happens. Fear of failure or mistakes is a normal part of the learning process, no matter how experienced the leader may be.

There's always an element of risk whenever we do something new. This is part of the excitement—you're on the edge. This fact is not to serve as a deterrent to risk taking, but an invitation to stretch, grow, and learn.

If you make a mistake or fail at something, stand back and "admire it," but don't dwell on it. Learn from it and move on. Without risk you simply will not grow and progress. And without growth and progress, how can you expect to make your dreams and goals a reality? It's like decision-making. If you don't make decisions you won't make any mistakes (other than not making the decision!) But you won't move on either. If someone has never failed at anything important, it is probably because they have shied away from doing new things and making significant decisions. I wouldn't believe anyone who tells you they have never failed at anything. They just may not want to admit their mistakes, either to themselves or you!

While excellent leaders have self-confidence, vision, and character, they learn from experience—both their victories and their defeats, making lots of mistakes as they go along, and by facing adversity. You'll learn your best lessons of leadership through your experiences of leading others. You need to do *whatever it takes,* which often means having the necessary courage to take risks.

Conscientious leaders consistently reflect on what's happening or what has happened so they can profit from their mistakes and failures. Reflecting is often neglected when things are going smoothly, but this may be a mistake.

There is an old cliché, "If it isn't broken, don't fix it." But this isn't necessarily good business practice. If something or someone can be helped to grow *before* they are broken—causing a halt or slow-down in productivity—wouldn't that be more effective? Reflect constantly so you learn to take action, perhaps a risk, to correct a situation before things break down. Here's a new cliché for leaders, *"If it isn't broken, make it better!"*

A leader needs to avoid getting bogged down in the negative circumstances that occur from time to time. Non-leaders tend to dwell on negative results and remember them longer and stronger than positive ones. Leaders, however, need to not allow negatives to disrupt their positive thinking. Instead they analyze and learn from them and move on.

Leaders Have a Strong Desire to Realize Their Dream

As I mentioned before, desire is another important ingredient of leadership. Who has desire? We all do! In fact we're born with it. Newborns have a desire for love, comfort, warmth, and nourishment, but they may lose some of it as they mature. An early negative environment, lack of nurturing, or a lack of positive leadership can jade their desire as they grow. They may change their focus from desire to survival.

How Is Your Drive?

Your drive is fueled by your desire and, at the same time, you need to satisfy it. However, you may need to harness your drive if it is leading you to excessive stress and endangering your health. Controlled drive is needed for steady progress and such control helps you to avoid "the flash in the pan" experience of pushing too hard and burning out quickly.

Some people with too strong a drive tend to be aggressive and "run over" anything or anyone who they perceive to be in their way or who isn't meeting their expectations. Aggressive behavior, however, will only drive people away. Be gently assertive in leading others. Be uplifting, kind, and caring. As the saying goes,

"You can't push a rope, but you can gently pull a wet noodle." Treat most folks as wet noodles, and you won't offend them.

The Trust Factor

Superb leaders have character. They gain and sustain trust because of their ability and willingness to be congruent in their vision and actions. They say what they mean and mean what they say. If they err in their talk and actions, they are the first to apologize and clarify the situation. They can be depended on for encouragement and support.

Above all, they have integrity. They keep their promises even in the face of adversity, mistakes, circumstances, and failures. Integrity is adherence to a code of values like sincerity, honesty, and trustworthiness. Who would want to follow a person who couldn't be trusted? No one. If you talk about your vision and mission but you don't follow through and your actions result only in short-term or minimum results, your integrity will be diminished. People will be hesitant to believe what you say and less inclined to follow your lead. You will need to earn their trust back through committed follow through.

Leaders Attract Leaders

Leaders attract people with leadership qualities, i.e., integrity, trust, character, and values, to their organization. This enables the organization to grow and prosper for the benefit of all. *To attract leaders you need to be a leader.*

The Platinum Rule

Leaders live by the Golden Rule—"Do unto others as you would have others do unto you." They then go a step further and live by the Platinum Rule—"Do unto others as they would want to be done unto." True leaders always do their best to treat others with respect, dignity, fairness, and appreciate who they are and what they do.

Leaders Go the Extra Mile to Understand Others

True leaders make every effort to understand people, respect them as unique individuals, and know where they're coming from. They realize effective communication occurs only when they do it on the other person's level of reception. They look at people as if they have "WII-FM?" (What's In It—For Me?) stamped on their foreheads. Broadcast your communications on "radio station" WII-FM so people can receive you!

True leaders also look at people as if they have MMFI (Make Me Feel Important) printed on their clothing. Help people to feel important and that there's something in it for them, and they're more likely to want to follow you.

Build Leaders

We build new leaders by building their self-confidence, giving them responsibility, and understanding their needs, wants, differences, and individuality. Encourage them to take risks and accept mistakes and failures as great opportunities to learn and fine-tune what they're doing. People should not be punished for their honest mistakes. Work with them to review the situations, then move on. Sincere understanding and positive reinforcement assures people that mistakes can be considered as part of the price of risk-taking.

The Results of Exemplary Leadership

When you lead people correctly and completely, your new generation of leaders will develop several attributes to guide them:

- ◆ They will have little or no fear of failure or mistakes.
- ◆ They will take risks.
- ◆ They will have character—integrity, trust, wisdom, and values.
- ◆ They'll consistently be enthusiastic, day in and day out.
- ◆ They will understand what causes them to have good "luck." As you'll recall, LUCK can be thought of as an acronym for Leadership, Understanding, Communications, Knowledge.
- ◆ They will have a vision that leads to a mission, which becomes the fabric of all they do in their business or career.

- They will regard change as an opportunity for growth.
- They won't take themselves too seriously and will have a good sense of humor about the periodic goofs.

Lead With a Positive, Humble Attitude

As a leader, or aspiring leader, you need to wear many "hats"—the most decisive being your attitude. It must, of course, be positive through and through in all facets of who you are. It doesn't matter whether business or pleasure is concerned, with your positive attitude you will overcome any other shortcomings you may have. There's a lot of negativity in this world and whatever it takes, you need to think positive for yourself, those you lead, and all who are affected by your attitude.

Your leadership can be the catalyst for the success of many people, and you need to humbly wear its mantel. Your people will love and respect you for your humbleness! The effects of your humble dedication to helping and your unwavering commitment to your principles and values will light the way for many who now live in the darkness of despair. You'll have the opportunity to care about them and encourage them to greatness.

Chapter Fourteen

The Law Of Cause And Effect

"Nothing happens until first a dream."
Carl Sandburg

Actions Cause Reactions

The law of cause and effect is similar to a law in physics—"For every action there is an equal and opposite reaction."

For example, a positive, loving attitude is the cause of a positive, loving effect; conversely, a negative, uncaring attitude is the cause of a negative, uncaring effect. We get what we "dish out."

It is unmistakable that for every effect, i.e., result, there's a cause for it—a reason why it happened that particular way. For example, say your business or career is going great. The cause could be from many factors, such as your leadership, your above-average dedicated associates, a strong economy, your excellent reputation, or your high-grade products or services, and opportunity. But there are *always* causes.

The opposite is true if your business or career is not going well. The cause could be from any or a combination of the following: your inadequate leadership, associates who lack enthusiasm and knowledge, a weak economy, a poor reputation, or slipshod production of products or provision of services. This may all appear simplistic, but it is real and worthy of consideration.

You are rewarded, or not, in accordance with the action you take or don't take (the cause) and the consequences (effect) you experience. You have free will and may act as you choose; you have that right. But you simply cannot escape the inevitable consequences of your action or inaction. You alone are responsible for your own actions and their effects, even if you did something (or not) at the request or suggestion of another person.

As mentioned before, set aside a definite period of time for thinking and planning every day. Think about how or what you need to do to change challenging circumstances you're experiencing to achieve positive outcomes. Also, consider what effect your actions could have, not only on your desired results but also on those who are assisting you in reaching your goals and those you are helping to do the same. Always, no matter what, strive to create win-win results where everyone concerned benefits, and no one loses. That's a mark of a true leader.

Do your best to look at yourself impartially and realistically and appreciate that you are a distinct and diverse individual with virtually unlimited potential for growth and success. By honestly observing the effect (result) of what you've created in your life and your business or career, you will notice that the cause very much revolves around you, your perceptions, beliefs, attitudes, and the actions you took or failed to take.

Are You Associating With Positive Thinking People?

Be careful in choosing your associates and friends. Your association with other forward thinking people who are also moving on is key to your success. Be sure to associate with and learn from the successful and positive thinking people in your industry. At times you will meet those who are struggling because of their negative attitude. Be the one to help them turn their attitude around. This will help you make your journey more significant and rewarding as you help others do the same.

How's Your Environment?

Your environment is more influential in your journey of success than your heredity, so look at it objectively. Is it contributing to or detracting from your efforts to achieve your dreams? If not, you may need to change your environment in order to realize your dreams and goals and those of your family. For example, if you need to have a quiet area to make your telephone calls, you may need to rearrange your environment to accommodate you better. What else could you change about your environment to support your success?

Will You Make the Necessary Changes to Succeed?

Are you willing to do *whatever it takes* to implement the necessary changes? Efforts such as continuing education and mentorship to improve your knowledge, skills and motivation level; association with more positive thinking people; and changing your vocation to one better suited to your personality, interests, and achievement of your dreams may be necessary. Above all, learn to love or better love and care about people. Remember that as was quoted earlier, when you help enough other people get what they want, you'll get what you want!

How Cause and Effect Relates to Being a Parent

The following poem (author unknown, Xoces, Inc.) expresses the relevance of cause and effect in a parent's life...

To Children's Parents

There are little eyes upon you
And they're watching night and day;
There are little ears that quickly
Take in everything you say.

There are little hands all eager
To do everything you do;
And children who are dreaming
Of the day they will be like you.

You're the children's idol;
You're the wisest of the wise.
In their little mind, about you
No suspicions ever rise.

They believe in you devoutly,
Hold that all you say and do,
They will say and do it your way,
When they are grown up, just like you.
There are wide-eyed little children
Who believe you're always right;
And their ears are always open
And they watch day and night.

You are setting an example
Every day in all you do;
For the children who are waiting
To grow up and be like you.

What's the Relationship of The Law of Cause and Affect and Money?

Let's touch briefly on the law of cause and effect as it relates to your ability to earn money. Let's take the commonly held belief that "money is the root of all evil." This phrase, which is probably familiar to you, is just not true. The correct phrase is, "the *love* of money is *a* root of evil (italics are mine)." See how easily ideas can be misquoted and misunderstood, as a result?

Some say, "Money won't buy happiness," but you may want to remind them that earning and possessing money has been accompanied by more happiness than has poverty. Money is the only thing that does what it does! Among other things, it buys a warm home, enough to eat, a college education, independence and dignity during retirement, not depending on your children or others for financial support, financial freedom, and a means to help others not as fortunate as you.

Money is available but you have to generally earn it. Very few people have significant sums of money handed to them without working for it. There are two ways to earn money: 1) People at work, or 2) Money at work. Most people earn it by working— either for someone else or as an independent business owner. (Although it's becoming more and more common to do both these days.) But we all need to remember that they need to do the work first. Many have this reversed: "Give me the money and then I'll do the work." This perception causes failure.

You are the cause of earning money, which is the natural effect of your work. *You* strive to earn the amount of money *you* want to provide the things *you* need and want to live the lifestyle *you* choose. Say you're not happy with the amount of money you're currently making. You may want to be totally financially free, so you have more choices in your life.

There are many obstacles on the road to the realization of this or any other big dream, and you need to do your best at all times to overcome them. You need to be focused and productive and make whatever changes that may be necessary to achieve this or any other goal or dream. You need to be the *cause* of it happening so you can enjoy the *effects!*

Restoring Zest in Your Life

Sometimes you may lose sight of the value of your work, and consequently, you may lose your zest for life, not just about your work, but about your life in general. Here are a few zest-restoring ideas that you can use now and every day:

♦ Understand that anything—your job, marriage, other relationships, and even your avocation—no matter how exciting it was in the beginning, can grow stale in time. You need to maintain your enthusiasm and have a positive attitude about everything. Once again, a continuing program of education and motivation can help you tremendously to stay fresh and excited.

♦ Keep in mind that you need to be creative to instill differences in your daily life. For example, try a new route to and from work, a different restaurant, a new hairstyle, sharing and rotating routine tasks at work and at home, and meeting and befriending new fun-to-be-around people. Eliminate the monotony of your routine by making some changes. Building enthusiasm into every day helps you to keep vitality in your performance and in your daily life.

♦ There is no such thing as a person without a future. Everyone has a future, and whether it is great or small will depend solely upon you. There are no small parts, only small actors. Dream big and work toward those dreams each day, step by step.

♦ See the "Big Picture" with you in it. See your life and your career or business in relation to the whole scheme of things. Remember that only you place limitations on yourself, regardless of what others might say or do. You have the say on what you do with your life and your goals. So do something exciting. Shed the shackles of boredom. Go for your biggest dream!

♦ Finally, continue to develop your ability to see yourself, your career or business, and whatever else you do through the eyes of the most important people in your life—family members, business associates, personal friends, and the community. This will help you realize that your life really matters and that you're already making a positive difference in many ways.

Keep your zest for life, and life will keep its zest for you.

If It Is To Be, It's Up To Me!

*"If you don't do it...
You'll never know
What would have happened
If you had done it."
So...
GO DO IT!*

If

"If you can keep your head when all about you
Are losing theirs and blaming it on you;
If you can trust yourself when all men and women
doubt you, but make allowance for their doubting too;
If you can wait and not be tired by waiting,
Or, being lied about, don't deal in lies,
Or, being hated, don't give way to hating,
And yet don't look too good, nor speak too wise;

If you can dream—and not make dreams your master;
If you can think—and not make thoughts your aim;
And, oh God, if you can meet with triumph and
disaster and treat those two imposters just the same;
If you can bear to hear the truth that you've spoken
Twisted by knaves to make a trap for fools,
Or see all the things you gave your life to broken,
And stoop and build them up with wornout tools;

If you can make one heap of all your winnings
And risk it on one turn of pitch-and-toss,
And lose, and start again a new beginning
And never breathe a word about your loss;
If you can force your heart and your severs and your
sinews to serve their turn long after they are gone,
So hold on when there is nothing in you—nothing!
Except the Will which says, "Oh God: Hold on;"

If you can talk with crowds and keep your virtue,
Or walk with kings and yet not lose your common
touch; if neither foes nor loving friends can hurt you;
And if all men and women count with you, yet none
too much; if you can fill each unforgiving minute
With 60 seconds' worth of distance run—
Then yours is the Earth, and everything that's in it,
And—which is more—you will be a Man or a
Woman. My sons, my daughters, God indeed made
you different—be sure you take advantage of it.
God bless you."

An adaptation of Rudyard Kipling's poem,
as embellished by Dave Yoho

About The Author

Tom Smith was raised in New Jersey in the U.S. He served in the United States Coast Guard during World War II. After graduating from Leicester College in Massachusetts, he held two sales positions before starting a successful 34 year career with a major insurance company.

As an agent, sales manager, and agency manager, Tom was awarded a President's Citation in each position. He has earned over 55 awards for excellence in sales and leadership.

Active in professional, civic, and church affairs, Tom was president of two local trade associations, a member of the JC's, member of his local Lions Club, and served as an elder and clerk in church. He was also on the board of directors and served as campaign chairman and chief volunteer officer of his local United Way Organization.

Tom has appeared on TV and radio talk shows and has been the featured speaker at various civic and business organizations including the members and donors of the local YMCA, The Florida International Club, and a leading financial services organization at their annual meeting.

Tom is married with two children and five grandchildren. He divides his time between homes in New Jersey and Florida.

NOTES

NOTES